The ESL Classroom

Teaching, Critical Practice, and Community Development

BRIAN D. MORGAN

UNIVERSITY OF TORONTO PRESS
Toronto Buffalo London

ISBN 0-8020-4334-8 (cloth)
ISBN 0-8020-8154-1 (paper)

Printed on acid-free paper

Canadian in Publication Data

Morgan, Brian D., 1956–
    The ESL classroom: teaching, critical practice, and community development

    Includes bibliographical references.
    ISBN 0-8020-4334-8 (bound) ISBN 0-8020-8154-1 (pbk.)

    1. English language – Study and teaching as a second language.* I. Title.

    PE1128.A2M673 1998   428'.0071   C98-930898-7

Pages 27–40 originally published as 'Teaching the Gulf war in an ESL classroom.' (1992/1993, Winter). *TESOL Journal*: 13–17. Copyright © 1993 TESOL. Revised with permission.
Pages 41–62 originally published as 'Public language, cultural authority, and the changing world of work.' *TESL Talk* 21: 141–59. Copyright © Queen's Printer for Ontario. Used with permission.
Pages 63–82 originally published as 'Identity and intonation: Linking dynamic processes in an ESL classroom.' *TESOL Quarterly* 31 (3): 431–50. Copyright © 1997 TESOL. Revised with permission.
Appendix 1 courtesy of *The Guardian Weekly*. Used with permission.

University of Toronto Press acknowledges the financial assistance to its publishing program of the Canada Council and the Ontario Arts Council.

The ESL Classroom

Teaching, Critical Practice, and Community Development

The complexities of teaching English as a second language to those newly arrived in Canada are addressed with insight and humour in this book. Brian Morgan draws extensively on his own teaching experience in Canada and in China to reinvestigate the nature and aims of ESL teaching and to formulate approaches to becoming a more effective ESL teacher.

Morgan's central principle is that ESL theories, materials, and approaches should be relevant to the social, political, and cultural conditions of each group of students. He stresses the importance of finding subject matter that will provide meaningful content for lessons, suggesting that discussion topics such as ecology, gender roles, changing social identity, and employment equity are often valid and appropriate for immigrant groups. Written for teachers by a teacher, the book includes lesson plans, examples of students' work, and vivid anecdotes of classroom incidents, presenting an important new perspective on ESL teaching.

BRIAN MORGAN is an ESL instructor, curriculum consultant, and teacher trainer for the Toronto Chinese Community Services Association and the Toronto Catholic School Board.

Contents

Acknowledgments

The final form of this book has evolved through support, criticism, and suggestions from professors, colleagues, and students over the past five years. I am especially grateful to Professor Jim Cummins of the Ontario Institute for Studies in Education for his needed advice, encouragement, and educational vision, which have helped me considerably along the path to completion. Material from many courses at OISE is also interwoven in this work. My thanks go to Professors Patrick Allen, Normand Frenette, Monica Heller, Roxanna Ng, Paul Olson, Roger Simon, and Ed Sullivan. I would also like to acknowledge the many formative discussions, arguments, and collaborations I have had with those engaged in critical ESL pedagogy at OISE. Thanks go to Nuzhat Amin, Rhiannon Bury, Professor David Corson, Nambuso Dlamini, Lynn Earls, Doug Fleming, Tara Goldstein, Helen Harper, Awad Ibrahim, Helen Moore, Donna Patrick, Alastair Pennycook, Bonny Norton, Alice Pitt, Ryuko Kubota, Arleen Schenke, Perry Shearwood, Lisa Taylor, Shelley Taylor, Alan Thompson, and Kathryn Tiede.

Perhaps the most important source of inspiration has been the students at the Toronto Chinese Community Services Association and St. Steven's Community House in Toronto, Ontario. Their stories both enrich this book and continue to shape my curiosity as a teacher. As well, I am grateful to the many ESL colleagues who have shared their insights from the classroom. In particular, I wish to acknowledge Norman Beach, Gay Bell, Eileen Boxhall, Regina

Chan, Laureen Chu, Jennie Lai, Cindy Lam, Rita Lee, Anita Leung, Lisa Loong, Jennifer Reed, Candy Sin, Winnie Sinn, Susanna Tan, Joseph Waye, and Christina Yurchuk. I would also like to thank Leo Lynch and Paul Dillon of the Toronto Catholic District School Board of Toronto for their support and commitment to the professional development of their ESL teachers.

Several chapters, sections, and concepts have benefited from the careful reading and comments of friends and colleagues. They are Sarah Benesch, A. Suresh Canagarajah, Bonny Norton, and Esther Podoliak. My gratitude and apologies are also extended to the various journal editors, editorial assistants, and anonymous readers who have had to bear with my extravagances, passions, and oversights. Special thanks go to Ron Schoeffel, Anne Forte, and Philippa Matheson of the University of Toronto Press, my copy editor, William Wood, and the anonymous UTP reviewers.

Often critical practice and community development begin at home. My heartfelt thanks go to family and friends for reminding me of what is most important and how it should inform academic and professional life. To Grace and Leo, Ruth and Roy, the Morgans, Hrytzaks, and Beattys, my deepest gratitude. And finally, this book is dedicated to Allison and Sarah for their love, support, and patience.

THE ESL CLASSROOM
Teaching, Critical Practice, and Community Development

CHAPTER 1

Introduction: Key Concepts

Learning/Unlearning ESL

My own initial training as an ESL teacher served several important purposes. It satisfied my early assumptions about the nature of language and provided me with a body of abstract methods and techniques that might safely guide me past the various landmines of the classroom. Soon after, however, I found myself fumbling with questions from students that went beyond my limited canon and experiences. Moreover, I tended to view such moments as disrespectful challenges to my newly sanctioned authority. Usually, in these times of threatened confidence, I would call upon some greater authority: the 'latest' research, famous 'expert,' or in more desperate occasions, the 'ultimate truth' on language. These responses were not specifically intended to deceive or mislead my students. Rather, they seemed to suit my idea of what a teacher should do, say, and know in a classroom.

Later, during a stint as an EFL instructor in the People's Republic of China, chinks in my protective armour began to appear. Unfortunately, my first private impulse was to berate the 'wilful ignorance' of students who resisted when presented with my 'state-of-the-art' techniques to develop fluency. These methods, I assumed, were certain to work if only given a chance and a commitment. Of course, it didn't work out that way, and I then embarked upon an unsettling adventure of listening to my students as much as telling them what to do. This proved more fruitful, and while I didn't always agree with them or comply with all of their requests, I started to gain a sense of their expectations and their histories, which informed their goals in learning.

As our classes together improved, my belief in the pre-eminence of my training and world-view seemed less resolute. English could no longer be thought of as a heritage monument, ready to be taken apart brick by brick and later faithfully and systematically reconstructed without regard for local surroundings. Several forays into process writing and communicative approaches to language teaching were unsatisfying. Of the latter, the idea that experimentation with new language forms could facilitate acquisition came smack up against the social stigma of an incorrect public utterance. When I requested *performance* to measure *competence*, they requested scripts of dialogues to memorize for conversation class. In China, I began to find out that the degree of individual experimentation I felt was intrinsic to a communicative activity was often considered inappropriate by my students.[1]

For my students, the contexts were numerous and complex. In spite of linguistic theory, an incorrect utterance was rarely seen as positive evidence of an expanding grammatical capacity. Rather, it was a sign of error and shame that often inhibited future participation. Also, the expression or invention of controversial ideas could result in unfortunate consequences for students within the shifting status quo of Chinese society. In this light, it was understandable how a scripted text, attributed solely to the foreign instructor, would be the preferred lesson plan of the day. But to ascribe political expediency as the primary motivation here is somewhat presumptuous. In spite of my preferences, rote learning was, and continues to be, a beneficial approach to language acquisition for some of my students.

Amongst the foreign teaching community at the university, the silence that greeted our latest communicative innovations was not appreciated. For some, it served to explain the underdevelopment of the Chinese economy. Other somewhat more charitable views depicted the situation within the popular explanatory realm of exoticism and inscrutability. In reality, we were all projecting our own language suppositions upon our students. There were also glaring points of hypocrisy in our comparative evaluations. While we criticized the Chinese political system for its silencing of our students' expressiveness, we ignored the exclusionary 'bureaucratese' that characterized our most powerful social institutions back home. Similarly, we smirked at political cadres and criticized the amount of time 'wasted' on political study, but we rarely reflected upon our country's internationally high percentage of lawyers in positions of institutional power. Nor did we consider the excessive and often exclusive forms of contractual entanglements that are a consequence.

With the assistance of my Chinese students, I tried to rethink ways of presenting English language materials to them. Their responses, unique in my experience, forced me to question my belief in an unassailable body of universal methods and materials (see Pennycook 1989). It was this lived contradiction that initiated other fruitful enquiries: Which social interests precipitated my desire to search for fixed solutions in prescribed methods? Why did my own personal experiences and strategies, learned first-hand, seem less legitimate? Understanding these questions is an ongoing task and one that links the ESL classroom with forms and processes of social authority specific to Western society. Our need to create 'new' theory, render 'old' techniques obsolete, and postulate 'scientific' methods without qualification – particularly from within the pressures and privileges of the Western academy – are very much a part of our unquestioned strategies in the classroom. Such strategies should be carefully scrutinized for their appropriateness in any classroom, especially ones of great social and cultural diversity.

This sense of going beyond a fixed body of methods and techniques, responding to the needs of a specific group of students, particularly when their values challenge your own, all the while questioning one's own assumptions, is what I now see as the most important approach to being an ESL teacher. At the same time, I feel that ESL teachers should not limit themselves to simply pondering biases and regretting their unfortunate consequences. Along with recognition, I believe, come other responsibilities. In addition to teaching language structure, we might explore how language is used to *structure* expectation, participation, and exclusion in our society. Such an approach actively encourages social advocacy and critical thinking as central to language curricula and is inspired by what Simon has defined as a 'Pedagogy of Possibility': 'Teaching and learning must be linked to the goals of educating students: to understand why things are the way they are and how they got to be that way; to critically appropriate forms of knowledge that exist outside of their immediate experience; to take risks and struggle with ongoing relations of power from within a life affirming moral culture.' (1988, 2).

The scope of a critical ESL pedagogy is indeed quite challenging and provocative. I do not see this approach as a replacement, but rather as a complement to what has already been developed for the ESL classroom. The ideas and lessons in this book are intended to help prepare students for a social world in which language practices can *deny* as well as provide opportunity. It is through such an awareness that newcomers might better develop the language skills necessary to act in their best interests and contribute effectively in the development of a more equitable and tolerant society. The following sections are intended to illustrate what a critical ESL pedagogy might offer and explore why these perspectives have been, to date, largely neglected in the second-language field.

Why Is Critical Language Teaching Underrepresented in ESL?

Many ESL teachers would reject considerations of social power or social conflict as appropriate for the ESL classroom. 'Our priority is to teach English, not politics' or 'I don't feel it's my place to bring up controversial topics' would be the common refrains. Such responses reflect a belief that schools are 'neutral' in regards to social mobility. That is, schools provide, but never deny, opportunity. Many writers concerned with education offer alternative perspectives (see Cummins 1996; Simon 1992; Giroux 1988; Shor 1992, McLaren 1989; Weiler and Mitchell 1992). Hardly neutral, educational institutions value specific forms of knowledge over others – an unquestionably *political* act when considering the diverse experiences of culture, race, gender, and class in our communities.

My own public-school education in Regina, Saskatchewan, is quite illustrative. Although Regina has one of the largest urban populations of aboriginal people in Canada, they were virtual strangers in our neighbourhood and especially our classrooms. Today, due to the rigorous tutelage of my former teachers, I can walk down the street identifying Corinthian, Doric, and Ionic columns, remember obscure dates from European antiquity, and resuscitate broken French phrases from the audiolingual experiments of Grade 8. In contrast, I have nothing to recall from my schooling of the rich cosmologies, economies, and languages of the aboriginal people of my home. For First Nations children, this glaring absence could only serve to actualize and personalize the cultural subordination and assimilation intended by institutional authority (see Cummins 1996, 9–14).

Similar to schools, language is conventionally perceived as neutral in the exchange of information or ideas (see Benesch 1991, 1994). ESL teachers who look at language critically or select politically controversial materials for the classroom are seen as introducing bias or propaganda into their teaching practices – they have 'agendas.' The appearance of 'neutrality' is also conspicuous in many ESL syllabus designs (see Nunan 1988). In evaluation and practice, issues of social conflict and how they might be embedded in discourse are usually secondary or forgotten in our language hierarchy, particularly with lower-level classes. The irony, of course, is that the prioritizing of structures and functions is itself a form of propaganda that regulates our students' expectations and social participation in ways of which we are often unaware.

A few years ago, I remember substitute teaching for a high-basic ESL class at a community centre. The regular teacher wanted me to review a specific verb tense and left an assignment sheet for the class. The sheet contained a paragraph focused on the tense with reading comprehension questions following. The story portrayed the working relationship of a doctor and a nurse. Shortly into the lesson, one obviously bored student asked, 'Are there

jobs in Canada?' It threw me off at first, but then I thought about
it and realized how inappropriate this subject material must seem.
Here were people struggling to find jobs during a recession and
I was giving them a grammar exercise based on the comfortable
and successful lives of health professionals. Other students joined
in and the lesson shifted towards their concerns. One student
told me that he had offered to work for free in an occupation
in which he had ten years experience. He was turned down. For
many students, this seemingly innocuous narrative only served to
reinforce feelings of frustration and helplessness. Ironically, the
prioritizing of 'neutral' structure over meaningful content, in this
case, served to inhibit the very acquisition that had formed the
basis of the teaching strategy.

The second point I want to raise is a perception amongst practitioners that critical theory is too abstract or jargon-filled to be of
any use outside of academic contexts. Elsewhere (Morgan 1997a),
I have argued that publishing activities in ESL can actually contribute to the perceived irrelevance of critical theory for practice.
Many teaching journals and 'in the classroom' sections of more
general publications place restrictions on length and focus that
allow for little beyond the description and sequencing of conventional methods and materials. Such spatial constraints, in particular, discourage critical analyses of the underlying paradigmatic
and ideological assumptions from which conventional methods
logically derive. Without the opportunity to articulate an alternative paradigm – or the conditions that might justify one – submis-
sions pertaining to critical ESL pedagogy can appear to take place
in a theoretical vacuum or to be ungrounded in the foundations
of the profession and thus, in both instances, unpublishable in the
eyes of certain editors. This view is not entirely without justification and suggests one important reason for writing this book: to
help bridge the specialized discourses that distance critical theorists from the experiences of ESL practitioners.

But there is more here than mere problems with specialized
language. 'New' ideas can be threatening. They mean investments
in time and challenges to existing practices for often overworked
and underpaid staff. Many ESL instructors receive no paid

professional-development time and must maintain certain attendance levels or lose their jobs. Such conditions discourage trying out innovations in the classroom. And to aggravate the situation further, practitioners sometimes become overly dismissive of academic research because they resent the privileged positions and salaries that theorists enjoy as ESL 'experts.'

There is no simple solution to the inherent contradictions here. Researchers, even if they do critical work, *are* part of a system that reproduces social power. Academic knowledge is as much an acquisition of exclusive and specialized codes – learning *how* to talk like an academic – as it is a representation of the 'discovery' of useful information. At the same time, the university represents one of the few places left to devote the time and resources needed to develop new ideas for education and enhanced possibilities for social life.

The third major point regarding the lack of critical ESL teaching pertains to the history and formation of Teaching English as a Second/Foreign Language. Within the general field of English Language Training, it is grudgingly recognized that the emergence and formalization of language training as a profession largely neglected the social sciences, instead directing research and specialization towards the areas of linguistic description, cognitive acquisition, and psycholinguistics. Such research priorities privileged a conceptual separation of language structure from social and historical contingencies. Language theory and its methodological applications became *universalized*, reinforcing a hierarchy of authority and expertise where university researchers discovered 'truths' about language and classroom 'technicians' dutifully applied such findings irrespective of their appropriateness for local conditions.

As suggested by Phillipson (1992), the professionalization of ELT and its basic tenets and priorities was neither accidental nor unanticipated. The decisions to disconnect language expertise from local contexts were motivated by underlying political and economic considerations: specifically, developing nations would continue to depend on Anglo-American interests to provide and define the terms of English Language Training deemed necessary to 'modernize' and participate successfully in a globalized economy (see also Canagarajah in press; Cooke 1987; Nayar 1997; Pennycook 1994a). I would argue that similar types of dependency relations have been transposed upon national and regional language planning. The current impetus to formulate national-second language standards and curricula implicitly sustains the notion that language performance and classroom practices can be 'scientifically' and systematically measured and evaluated – and subsequently funded or terminated – regardless of the unique sociocultural conditions and needs of each local community.

What is Critical Language Teaching?

Here are some key concepts and examples that have inspired the lesson plans in this book.

1) Critical thinking is more than a topic, function, or language sub-skill: 'critical thinking ... should be integral to all aspects of the curriculum' (Cummins 1989a, 75). Accordingly, critical language educators might ask questions that go beyond 'what works' and 'how can I do things more efficiently?' Examples might be questions such as:
  a) Why and how did the syllabus get organized this way?
  b) What social values and whose interests are supported or excluded?
  c) What are the possibilities for critical work within the existing conditions of my employment?

Question *1a* is a reminder that administrative models and funding have profound influence on language teaching and syllabus design. The decision to go with a graded, structural syllabus can reflect accounting requirements dictated by special government funding for job training. The program, of necessity, becomes highly quantitative: fixed time per fixed level, teaching dictated by examinations, percentages of passes and failures produced for auditing purposes, and so on. Other programs have precarious funding based upon arbitrary numbers of students. Most often, such programs can't afford to turn anybody away, so the classes become multilevel, with teachers discouraged from placing students with regular attendance in more suitable levels. In both examples, innovations or research in language have negligible influence on what actually happens in the classroom.

Administrative needs are not the only social values reflected in the curricula. I helped edit a set of ESL grammar materials organized around field trips. One of the chapters dealt with a major fast-food restaurant chain. After I read the chapter, I mentioned to the authors that the image given of the restaurant was entirely supportive, not unlike their own advertising campaigns. I pointed out that this organization was also criticized for its anti-union activities and had also been targeted for its excessive production of garbage. The first point was particularly important considering the high number of ESL students in low-paying, service-sector jobs. The authors agreed. They simply hadn't thought about it.

Their experience is one we all share. As teachers or as materials writers, we select from what is available in the public sphere. We are often 'unaware' of alternatives and dissenting points of view, because powerful institutions have the resources to project a singular image of themselves that comes to be accepted as all there is to know. The curriculum is naturally perceived as 'neutral' when other options and alternative perspectives are made invisible.

Once a teacher realizes the limitations of a particular syllabus, it is necessary to think about some of the reasons why it would still remain in place. Sometimes politics drives pedagogy; inappropriate programs may persist simply because certain agencies or bureaucracies need to be seen serving 'clients.' It is important to remember that the *appearance* of government services for newcomers is as important as the actual efficacy of delivery. The appearance, moreover, is crucial to how liberal-democratic societies reproduce social and political power. If newcomers 'fail' in Canada, social elites can deflect responsibility back upon the presumed 'deficiencies' newcomers bring with them. Given both the social and administrative constraints each teacher experiences, moments and places for critical teaching should reflect the possibilities of such work and the particular interests of the students and the local community.

2) Language does not simply report or transmit reality. Language 'conditions' our expectations and desires, and communicates what might be possible in terms of ourselves – our identity – and the 'realities' we might develop.

This does not mean that we are part of a helpless mass controlled by corporate and political wordsmiths. But neither are we autonomous; we do not come to knowledge entirely of our own 'free will.' We are instead 'subjects' *of* and *through* language (see Peirce 1995; Simon 1992; Weedon 1987; Cherryholmes 1988). Dominant social groups do rely upon the power of language to normalize ways of seeing, knowing, and doing that support their particular interests and privileges, but consent is never a foregone conclusion.

At times, individuals or minority groups have difficulties applying 'standard' meanings to the changing social conditions and inequalities that they experience. Dissenting meanings invariably emerge. It is at this juncture, according to poststructuralist theory, that language practices are most unstable and contentious – contentious because dominant social groups rely upon the power of language to mobilize 'common-sense' ways of seeing, knowing, and doing that support their privileges.[2] In sum, language is not something that 'sits on the sidelines' during the struggle over competing social interests and access to material resources. Language is used to put people in their place and people use language to change the place in which they have been put (see Clark et al. 1990, 1991; Corson 1993; Janks 1993; Morgan 1996a, 1997b).

3) Students have social needs that are often interdependent with language needs. Successful lessons occur when critical language skills are organized as a complement to genuine social concerns and community priorities.

This is a key organizing principle for a community-based ESL program and comes in response to the historical separation of ESL theory and methodology from the local social contexts where

instruction takes place. In terms of lesson planning, social issues and community concerns are often the starting point from
which to generate lessons. As well, the cultural, political, and
linguistic practices that form communities or threaten their cohesion provide key issues on which to focus (see Ashworth 1985;
Auerbach and McGrail 1991; Stern 1997). Assessment is not restricted to linguistic criteria, but incorporates the evaluation of
social tasks: resolving a local problem or actively participating in
public decision-making. By conceptualizing a 'language' lesson in
this way, I would argue that teachers are able to generate unique
language strategies that would otherwise elude more systematic
approaches to second language acquisition (SLA). For example,
in the chapter on teaching the Gulf War, one of the lesson plans
involved bringing my adult students into a Grade 7 classroom to
talk about their lived experiences of warfare. To prepare for this
activity, my students generated a set of questions they wanted
to ask the Grade 7s. In fact, these 'questions' were unique to the
moment and context. They were intended not just to inquire, but
to persuade, to inform, and to caution. They were multifunctional
speech acts subsumed within an 'interrogative' surface structure
that enabled other rhetorical intentions to occur. Most importantly, the pedagogical strategy of 'making questions' became inseparable from my students' particular experiences and concerns
as parents, community members, and survivors of warfare.

4) *Students are not just entering a new culture of holidays, sports,
and food. They are also entering a new culture of politics, employment,
education, and family life. What can be said? What can be insinuated
or challenged? Who may speak with authority? Students enter a social
world where sophisticated forms of exclusion persist.*

To talk *with* a businessman, an academic, or an artist, you are
usually required to talk *like* them if you want to be taken seriously
or get what you need. Each of these areas – some more than others
– has a specialized language that carefully 'polices' itself, particularly the degree to which it can be demystified and challenged
from without. The reasons are not surprising. If everyone could

talk like an economist, for example, their 'value' (i.e., salaries and status) would diminish accordingly and they would be subject to greater public scrutiny.

We can say that certain areas and institutions of society are governed by 'discourses,' a term I associate closely with the work of the philosopher Michel Foucault (see Cherryholmes 1988; Pennycook 1994b). In describing Foucault's notion of discourse, McLaren states that discourses 'govern what can be said and what must remain unsaid, who can speak and who must listen' (1989, 180).[3] The importance for ESL students is that they are often confronted by unfamiliar discourses when they seek employment, or government services, or talk to their children's teachers and to their local politicians. ESL syllabuses routinely include functions and notions such as 'making requests,' 'giving information,' 'seeking confirmation,' and 'formal relationships.' Less likely are they to include a set of functions and notions that might be under a heading such as English for Self-Defence. In terms of discursive knowledge, such a list might include 'seeking or avoiding responsibility,' 'identifying and using jargon,' 'silencing or encouraging dissent,' 'ambiguity,' 'dismissiveness,' and so on.

5) What is or is not a 'critical' perspective is very much contingent on time, place, and the particular experiences of students. For some students, the ability to read politics 'between the lines' is a 'traditional' or familiar literacy skill.

When our class and the Grade 7s met during the Gulf War lessons, an interesting tension developed between the classroom teacher and a couple of my students. Whenever my students started discussing personalized experiences from childhood (e.g., bad food, hiding from bombs), the Grade 7 teacher would challenge them and steer the discussion towards issues of global politics, competing ideologies, and historical conflicts. She actually was quite upset.

The key point is that in this specific context, firsthand accounts of daily life during a war detracted from the depiction of the war as a necessary conflict between 'good' and 'evil.' In this context, my students' personal stories broke down the borders between 'them' and 'us' and thus became highly *political*, actively democratic, and profoundly challenging to the ways in which consent is sometimes arbitrarily mobilized in societies. Several students noted and discussed the contextual politics involved when we went back to our own room. Their comments made me aware that ESL students may already see and read things in ways that a teacher perceives to be 'critical' or of higher order literacy skills. Moreover, the priorities that a critical educator establishes for a class may inadvertently represent established forms of authority for some students.[4]

6) It is often how *we teach rather than* what *we teach that creates difficulties in the classroom. So, we shouldn't readily assume what is or isn't contentious in critical language work.*

I can recall one potentially disruptive situation that occurred during a lesson about violence against women. I was introducing some excellent ESL materials on the subject produced by the Ontario Ministry of Citizenship when one male student vehemently stated that the lesson was a waste of time because his culture 'didn't do this kind of thing.' At this point an argument about whether or not one's culture was violent against women would only lead to resentment, anger, and possible withdrawal from the class. Instead of arguing over the merits of the lesson, I decided to change the *context* in which the lessons would be evaluated. The perceived uselessness or insensitivity of the materials, by one student, became foregrounded as part of the class activity. First, I asked the class to evaluate the advice put forth in the article. How would it be received in their specific cultural communities? Where was it useful? Where was it useless for their specific community? How could it be improved? In this way, the students could approach the materials as experts and cultural mediators rather than potential abusers from an 'inferior' culture. The resulting discussion raised many important issues and perspectives that were of benefit for the *entire* class.

7) In critical language teaching, students' experiences and expecta-
tions are central to the ongoing development and implementation of
the syllabus. This means not only affirming student 'voices,' but also
exploring opportunities where students can examine the social processes
and language practices that may form their identity. This involves Paulo
Freire's concept of 'problem-posing' (see Auerbach and Wallerstein
1987; Freire 1974; Wallerstein 1983; Shor 1992), creating opportunities
where 'common-sense' knowledge is examined in an 'uncommon' and
critical manner (Simon 1992, 1988).

In the chapter on a 'dangerous future,' many of the students, particularly women, stated that they had seldom participated in discussions on social issues that concerned them. When we started
exploring the situation more closely in class, it became apparent
that for many students the distance they felt from politicized debate was experienced as a *personal* inadequacy: they lacked the
necessary language skills to be taken 'seriously.' Problem-posing
enabled several students to consider another possibility: inadequacy might be an *intention* produced by the language that
framed political discussion in the community. Encouraging such
an awareness became a major focus of our lessons on reading
media accounts of global warming.

My experience has been that telling someone 'You're wrong'
or 'You must do this instead' can create mistrust and barriers to
further learning. Nonetheless, there are moments and situations
where I disagree with students and I try to state why certain social
values are important to me. Problem-posing involves circulating
probing questions and ideas in a thought-provoking manner that
engages rather than threatens people and opens up possibilities
for critical reflection. I don't believe teachers should dictate to
their students when and where to get involved in public decision
making. I do, however, believe teachers, through problem-posing,
can help students see issues in critical ways that promote their
participation. Instead of blaming themselves and withdrawing,
some students may decide to challenge the terms on which decisions are being made in their name.

8) Dialogic teaching is important for critical work. As we learn about our students, we learn about ourselves as well. As teachers and as citizens, we become aware of the things we take for granted, and how we reproduce these values in our day-to-day teaching.

In critical pedagogy, this idea has been closely identified with the adult-literacy work of Paulo Freire (1973, 1974). Freire emphasized that his students already had wisdom and invaluable experiences, unlike the image of helplessness and ignorance that often informed policy and curricula. An empowering educator would need to view students as equals and resist prescribing what empowerment is or should be for students and the community (see Cummins 1990; McLaren and Leonard 1993).[5] Once educators engaged in this dialogic process, they would come to understand themselves, their society, and the purposes of education in ways that were previously not comprehended. It is precisely through our interactions with alternative conceptual frameworks (e.g., other languages, literacy practices, values) that our attention can be drawn to the partiality of our knowledge and the potentially adverse social consequences that language practices, when taken for granted, hold for minority communities.

Freire's concepts of dialogic engagement and problem-posing are extremely important for this book. At the same time, it should be pointed out that critical reflection doesn't result in silence and inaction. Some teachers might feel that once we identify bias and discrimination in our own teaching, we no longer have the right to speak out or to criticize other social practices. In this sense, everything becomes relativized out of fear of unwittingly imposing yet another oppressive educational practice on minority students. But this would be contrary to Freire's own intentions and the spirit behind the lessons in this book. For Freire, dialogue and problem-posing are not just methods but means by which shared goals of social and political justice might be furthered (see McLaren and Leonard 1993; Weiler 1991). In the classroom, it's important to recognize differences based on culture, race, gender, sexual orientation, or age. But it's also important to identify and struggle to achieve collective goals and moral imperatives across boundaries of social identity. For teachers, it often requires taking sides on important issues and speaking honestly and explicitly about values that are important.

9) Critical language skills are important for the individual, the community, and the society.

Many believe, as does Saul, that 'criticism is the most constructive tool available to any society because it is the best way to prevent error' (1992, 8). Inevitably, when you teach people literacy or a second language, you must examine how meanings are socially constructed. As you teach your students, they may confront you with features and practices of your own society that you have not considered, and these features can be unpleasant, contradictory, or even blatantly hypocritical. But the benefits are tangible: with the development of critical language skills, a society is less likely to look back in tragic retrospect upon its silence and complicity. Instead, it might look towards the future with a modest degree of hope that the errors of the past will not be repeated.

Why Focus on Community?

In urban centres, language education takes place in major institutions such as universities and colleges. But it also thrives in smaller locales: community centres, church basements, staff rooms of hospitals, temporary spaces in malls, and so on. Newcomers often have many choices when they decide to join a program. Sometimes this choice is made on a strict evaluation of language criteria: which program teaches more grammar, more pronunciation, more speaking? Often, however, this choice is based upon an entirely different set of conditions: a student's familiarity with the delivery organization, friendships with other students, or a rare opportunity to get away from domestic responsibilities. The cumulative result of those who choose to stay in a program is a high degree of cohesiveness and collective identity that characterizes 'community.'[6] The key point is that many classes exist because of *social* reasons, and these reasons need to be brought to the foreground for effective language instruction to proceed.

Community is a highly resonant idea for language education. In a society that celebrates individuality and competition, the notion of community strongly suggests alternative claims to validity or priorities – what counts as knowledge – in the organization of language programming. Community rèminds us that the people we work with are not just *learners* – an isolating cognitive designation – but also *students*, a social term suggesting collective responsibilities.[7] Similarly, as we recognize the need for a flexible and adaptive mix of methods, materials, and assessment tools for different community contexts (see Allen 1983; Allen et al. 1990; Lynch 1996), we might also extend the notion of flexibility to the degree that we allow English to be taught as an isolated topic disconnected from social concerns. Whereas a class of aspiring young academics may need to learn more formal techniques of writing, a class of seniors might want to know more about the country and society to which they have come and be less concerned about error corrections in their second or third language. Community seems like a good place to start thinking about a more locally and socially responsive way of teaching ESL. It doesn't mean idealizing a vague social notion. It means sometimes examining conflicts and forms of abusive authority that flourish because of communal ties that bind like family. A community-based, critical ESL pedagogy doesn't mean neglecting language. It means organizing language around experiences that are immediate to students.

Teachers as Advocates

In the perspectives that I have sketched in this introductory chapter, it has been my intention to 'raise the stakes' and extend the traditional responsibilities of ESL teachers. What I propose here is that classroom teachers explore the possibilities of social advocacy, or active citizenship, as a potential area of growth (see Elson 1989; Ashworth 1985; Cooke 1993). The idea of advocacy can be somewhat disconcerting, particularly in a discipline that has historically separated itself from social and political concerns and has given limited autonomy to classroom teachers. For some, advocacy gives an impression of 'manning the barricades.' In reality, each program and each individual's skills and beliefs will influence the role that they explore as active citizens. Some teachers may get involved in petition writing and contacting elected officials; others may try to influence program administrators at their community agencies. Advocacy sometimes means speaking on behalf of your students, but it also means seeking out opportunities where they can speak for themselves and with the potential to influence decisions. All options can be explored.

There are two major reasons I see in support of an expanded teachers' role. First, ESL teachers are uniquely positioned in society to witness directly and assess the consequences of government policy for newcomers. On the one hand, this can mean the effects of legislative policy and political decisions pertaining to immigrants and refugees (see Burnaby and Cumming 1992, Podoliak 1993). On the other, it can also pertain to the 'hidden' effects of public policy that may not be anticipated by the authors. In the case of the Gulf War, for example, the government and media's depiction of events and the characterization of Saddam Hussein worried several of my students. What would happen to relations with Arabic and Muslim communities in Canada? As one of my Iranian students feared, the rhetorical language used to prepare for war was ambiguous and general enough that incidents of racism and potential violence against Arabic and Muslim communities might be encouraged. When such situations occur, ESL teachers are sometimes the first and only person that a newcomer confides in. It is not only a case of trust and close personal relationships, but also one of social mediation that causes students to seek out help from teachers. ESL teachers, through both their responses and their silence, define what is appropriate and what might be possible in a new country.

The second point in favour of increased advocacy also relates to our unique social proximity to our students and the insights we can gain from them. As mentioned above, newcomers are an invaluable resource in ways that are not so often clear or initially appreciated. Students react and respond to events and information in ways that not only surprise me, but also educate me. This is not to say that my students are necessarily more intelligent or experienced than other Canadians, but that they have not been integrated into the dominant values of the society to the same degree as long-term residents. The key point to make here is that we sometimes forget that we have inherited and *internalized* a set of values and common-sense assumptions, an ideological system, which can appear so natural to us that we are often unable to scrutinize our actions and beliefs critically, or reflect on the social interests that are privileged as a result. In this perspective, we might imagine the ESL classroom as a key location for a *shared* process of social development between a host country and its newest citizens. There are, I believe, limitless possibilities for such an expanded role. Either as observers, mediators, or social activists, ESL instructors have the potential to develop skills and insights that promote the aspirations of community development far beyond the local view.

Notes on Critical Practice

In the following chapters I will provide examples of lesson plans, teaching problems, and student work. A key pedagogical point to remember is that this type of work is contingent upon the specific circumstances of each teaching situation. In my own workplace, I have had considerable autonomy in developing my own syllabus and considerable support from the administrators in my program. I am required to maintain a certain number of students in attendance, however, or I will lose my job. This serves as a significant impetus to satisfy the needs, expectations, and pace desired by my students. I recognize that these conditions have made the presentation of controversial materials easier in some ways and uniquely circumscribed in others.

The class level for most of the following chapters is high-intermediate to advanced. Because of continuous intake in my program, a number of students fall outside of these designations. In the chapters on community policing and on identity and intonation, the general class ability was around an intermediate level.

For lower level teachers, I can't offer any direct examples of critical work. Hopefully, the lessons in this book can inspire teachers to develop critical language materials appropriate to their own classrooms.

CHAPTER 2

Teaching Politics in an ESL Classroom

Introduction

For many of us, politics is a haphazard event of casting a ballot, followed by marginal interest in the process of governance. At a past TESL conference, Kevin Moloney addressed this problem succinctly by noting that democratic rights are often regarded 'as if they fell from the sky' (Moloney 1991). There is little understanding of the past and current struggles that are essential for their attainment. Politics, as it affects most of our lives, rarely intrudes into personal discussions of physical survival. Accordingly, politics is perceived as only an occasional nuisance, distinctly separate from most areas of community life.

This limited concern with things political is not just a result of indifference or confusion, but also reflects a monocultural way of thinking, reinforced in our schools, about the obligations, rights, and practices of citizenship. We live and act within a particular *discourse* on citizenship. Who speaks with authority? When, where, and how can people respond? Many citizens remain passive because they feel it is appropriate, not just because they are apathetic.

As a discourse, the implicit rules of conduct do not necessarily serve all people equally. The poll tax for Chinese immigrants, the internment of Japanese and Ukrainian Canadians during wartime, and the exclusion of European Jews escaping the Holocaust are a few of the consequences of a socialized reluctance to challenge misguided policy in the history of Canada (Ng 1989). Exclusion-ary practices continue to this day, and it is common to see insti-tutional forms of discrimination such as between 'political' and 'economic' refugees, or Canadian and non-Canadian experience, pass before the public eye with minimal scrutiny of their arbi-trariness or consideration of the often tragic consequences.

For many ESL students, politics is a lived experience constructed in many different ways. For example, the willingness to engage in politicking might reflect a country of origin in which legal sta-tus, employment or living conditions are individually negotiated and rarely subject to impersonalized or institutional governance. When an ESL instructor nervously steers the discussion away from 'controversy,' that instructor risks negating language practices that have been central to students' strategic competence and motivation in their first language.

Preconceptions about what is or is not political have other po-tential problems for classroom practice. In many societies the language of politics, of necessity, is highly symbolic and covert. Our students, silenced in the conventions available to us, become highly adept in making and discerning meanings of which we may not be aware. As well, they will use forms of expression that we find apolitical to contest their social world. One recent example that intrigued me, particularly after my Chinese teach-ing experience, was the 'inadvertent' publication in China of a palindrome critical of the Chinese government. Composed in ma-trices, palindromes are multidirectional rhyming poems that in-corporate the basically monosyllabic and uninflected nature of the language (Elvin 1991, 59). As reported in the Western press, the above-mentioned political tract was so skilfully 'hidden' within the poem's structure that even the usually diligent censors were unable to notice it. Such unique, literate skills would certainly elude most Westerners, especially as a form of organizing political discourse.

A reversal of sorts was experienced by Maureen Hynes. While teaching in China, she introduced an article from *Time* magazine on how former North American radicals had become establish-ment business managers. Hynes' intention was to lead towards a discussion of the current activities of Red Guards from the Cultural Revolution – an issue that associates easily with the dynamics and compromises of political authority. Instead, she became bogged down in a laborious explanation of culturally bound symbols and meanings from the *Time* article. In her own words, 'apparently suitable materials can be totally inappropriate' (Hynes et al. 1982, 36). Hyne's experience is one I've had on several occasions. It underlines the problems that can occur when we make presumptions about 'political' materials and methods in the classroom.

A 'Grammar' of Politics

In spite of the difficulties of teaching politics in the ESL classroom, I don't believe its desirable or possible to avoid the issue. As I mentioned earlier, we should consider that ESL materials and methods are already 'political.' To a remarkable degree, our profession has historically constructed itself as a closed system: a body of theories, methods, and research techniques largely disconnected from the local contexts where language instruction takes place. As Phillipson (1992) has demonstrated, the decisions that formalized the English Language Training profession were made for political reasons. ELT was fashioned in a manner that encouraged and maintained relations of economic dependency to the benefit of Anglo-American interests. While on the surface such historical considerations may not seem immediate to the ESL classroom, I would argue that this legacy persists in many implicit and sophisticated ways in the profession (see also Canagarajah in press; Cooke 1987; Nayar 1997; Pennycook 1994a).

This does not mean that language teachers and researchers in applied linguistics are unaware of social and cultural contexts. Instead, I am suggesting that it is more an issue of *how* applied linguists have approached the notions of society, culture, or politics that is often problematic. Whereas philosophers might tend to think of language too philosophically or unsystematically, applied linguists might err towards rendering the human condition too linguistically – I dare say almost like a grammar: something frozen in time, form separated from complex interrelationships, its componants isolated and analysed, and then fixed within a universal model of structural relationships.

Krashen's work (1988) on second language acquisition provides an interesting illustration. Similar to most researchers in this area, Krashen relies on psychological concepts and categories in his research. For example, he identifies 'attitudinal' factors as having influence upon learning proficiency. Referring to research done by Gardner and Lambert (1972), Krashen distinguishes *integrative* motivation, 'the desire to be like valued members of the community,' from *instrumental* motivation, 'the desire to achieve proficiency in language for utilitarian, or practical reasons.' These motivational categories then are 'interrelated' with 'personality factors' such as empathy and self-confidence: 'Briefly, it is hypothesized that the self-confident or secure person will be more able to encourage intake and will have a lower filter. Traits relating to self-confidence (lack of anxiety, outgoing personality, self-esteem) are thus predicted to relate to second language acquisition ... The less self-confident person may understand the input but not acquire, just as the self-conscious person may filter (or avoid) in other domains' (1988, 23). The key point to be made here is that psychology's focus on the individual understates the causative role played by social and political conditions (see Bourne 1988, Peirce 1995). Constructed this way, research can only offer a partial view at best. Language learning appears to take place in a social vacuum. The conditions, histories, and conflicts that have precipitated anxiety, confidence, or a desire for prestige have been essentially obscured. Moreover, categories such as *anxiety*, *attitude*, and *personality* tend to focus judgement and responsibility on the atomized individual. That is, to borrow from Krashen, these categories place a conceptual 'filter' around the ESL student. In contrast, concepts such as *inequality* are forms of relationship that bring into focus group complicities and strongly indicate political contingencies rather than cognitive processes.

An alternative take on second language acquisition can be seen in Goldstein's study (1997). Goldstein found that individuals who participated in an English workplace program had to weigh

English language practices against linguistic codes of ethnic solidarity at work. As women in a patriarchal community, and as 'unskilled' labour in an inhospitable economy, first-language use at the worksite offered a limited but possible form of economic and social security. That this security may inhibit the acquisition of language skills for greater economic mobility is a lived contradiction that cannot be reduced to universal notions of utility. Of further note, in Goldstein's study, minority cultural forms of authority were used to quell challenges to larger institutional interests. In a successful battle to stop unionization, the employer brought in a priest who spoke the workers' native language to dissuade worker membership. Clearly, issues of gender, economy, and sociocultural experience should not be ignored in research on second language acquisition, nor should they be considered total strait-jackets upon people's lives. In Goldstein's study, individuals made choices to accept or deny the reciprocal obligations and privileges of their social group.

As ESL instructors, we are informed by a research tradition. It both anchors our suppositions when we search for answers and provides the starting point for our departures. In this perspective, our culturally defined understanding of language has informed many of our assumptions about politics and our responsibilities as educators. How then should we conceptualize teaching politics in an ESL classroom? Of greatest importance is an understanding that our own beliefs and values are not universal nor necessarily aspired to as organizing principles by others. In this perspective, we should promote greater diversity in our teaching strategies and show a willingness to explore 'unusual' ideas about political experience generated through dialogue with our students.

Teaching the Gulf War in an ESL Classroom

The Gulf War was a topic that I initially avoided in my ESL classroom. I recognize that my reluctance represented the confusion and contradictory feelings that I had for the war. Both my Jewish upbringing and an enjoyable stint working on a kibbutz in Israel have forged a bond with the state that makes it often difficult to be objective regarding the politics of the region. This encouraged my support for the forces aligned against Iraq. Furthermore, Saddam Hussein's conduct in the Iran–Iraq war and his attacks upon his Kurdish citizenry only underscored legitimacy for his removal. As someone who has lived, worked, and travelled in several Moslem countries, however, I found the depiction of events, histories, and beliefs simplistic and hypocritical. The sanctimony with which the mainstream Western press covered Iraq's invasion of Kuwait was all the more fraudulent when placed beside European colonial history in the Middle East.

In my ESL class, I was the one who usually steered the class away from issues surrounding the war. But the war was all around us and couldn't be avoided. Our adult ESL class takes place in a public school room provided by the local board of education. Some of my students actually have children attending classes in the same building. To their surprise and mine, the children started to exhibit posters about the war throughout the halls of the school. If there was a uniformity to the posters, it was that they were dominated by the hardware and technology of warfare. Similar to the press, there was no reflection of the reality of destruction and death. For my students, war and revolution had been lived tragedies causing many of them to come to Canada: World War II, the Japanese invasion of China, the Chinese Civil War, the Vietnam War, the Iranian Revolution, the Great Proletarian Cultural Revolution, and the war in El Salvador are their painful personal memories.

Next to our classroom, there was a large map of the Middle East that had been made and adorned under the direction of the classroom teacher. Festooned with tanks, soldiers, jet fighters and flags, the map included a rather terse history lesson: 'Saddam Hussein invaded Kuwait; the United Nations asked him to leave, but the dictator refused: the United Nations now has to free Kuwait.' One day, as she was stapling a few more tanks to the mural, the classroom teacher asked me how I liked their class project. I suggested that history had been treated rather briefly and that the students should have more of a background on the history and cultures of the region. She replied that her seventh-grade students were not that advanced and could only handle the 'facts.' A heated debate about the facts ensued.

The next day, I recognized an opportunity for my students and myself to deal with the war in a constructive way. I asked the teacher next door if she and her students would be interested in talking to my students about their personal experiences of war and revolution. She agreed, and then we made a date convenient for both classes.

When I approached my students with the idea, they had mixed feelings on one issue in particular; while most believed that their experiences and insights would be valuable to share, several students felt that their English abilities would prohibit them from contributing effectively. I was surprised at this response, because I had assumed that these advanced ESL students frequently used their new linguistic skills in their day-to-day life. Yet for many students, even those at an advanced level, school still remains the only place where English is spoken. One of the reasons is a cultural sense of identity where the structural form of public speech, if incorrect, devalues both the content of the utterance and the dignity of the speaker. How my students presented themselves in public was important to them and, in some ways, inseparable from what they intended to communicate (see Bell 1995). My students' concerns also made me realize how I have developed a way of filtering the spoken word, where judgement of content is rarely subordinated to the precision of form.

These were the emerging concerns that helped create the pedagogical strategy for my first lesson on the Gulf War. Each subsequent lesson was contingent upon the strengths and weaknesses of its predecessor.

LESSON 1: Forming questions and ideas for joint class on the Gulf War (approximately 2 hours)
The students were placed in groups of three to work together on the following questions written on the blackboard:

1) What are the most important ideas to present to the children? (Make a list)

2) What kinds of questions could you ask the students about their understanding of the Gulf War? (Make a list)
3) How does war change your day-to-day life?

Teacher's Note: Working in small groups with familiar people helped the students overcome silencing memories and better conceptualize the types of ideas and questions that they wanted to express. The preparation of questions for an ESL student helps emphasize the multifunctional possibilities in question formation. Questions can draw upon personal experience, or be limited to superficial items in a text. As well, questions can be framed to reflect favourably or negatively upon a subject. Questions can 'persuade' or 'coerce' while they 'inquire.' This is an important aspect, or meaning potential (see Chapter 4 on Halliday's concept of register), of grammar often neglected in the ESL classroom, particularly because it makes structural 'description' contingent upon social context – an unfamiliar strategy in many grammar lessons. As I moved from group to group, I also had a chance to guide students through problems with interrogative structure and the tense-aspect system. After about forty-five minutes, I brought the class back together to review their work and to place their lists on the board. Each student was asked to elaborate on his/her question or idea and to tell the class what information they hoped to encourage in the discussion.

Here is a complete list of the ideas produced by the class and placed on the blackboard:

1) Experience of bombing
2) Experience of being controlled by other people (foreigners/neighbours)
3) Causes of war and revolution
4) Shortages of food, water, medicine, etc.
5) Importance of knowledge can prevent bigger wars
6) Living between death and life
7) Knowledge of war = carelessness of human beings

The complete list of questions placed on the blackboard was as follows:

1) Where are Kuwait and Iraq?
2) What was the relationship between Iraq and Kuwait before the occupation of Kuwait?
3) Why did Iraq occupy Kuwait?
4) Do you think this will provide a good future for the next generation?
5) Why is the U.S. fighting Iraq?
6) What is the relationship between the Gulf War and Canada?
7) Why don't we buy oil from Iraq instead of Kuwait?
8) Why is the U.S. not afraid of Islamic jihad?

My students told many stories about the personal difficulties of trying to survive in wartime: the bad food, treacherous neighbours, constantly moving. One story stands out in my mind as a unique statement on wartime as experienced by a child. The speaker was a young resident of Hanoi during some of the worst bombing of the Vietnam War. She recalled how her father had taught her to know whether or not she was in danger of being killed during a bombing attack. 'If the bombs are straight above you,' she said, 'then you're safe because they're flying past you. If they're behind you, then you'd better run and hide.'

LESSON 2: Reading two short stories (approximately three hours)

Teacher's Note: To provide ideas for a future composition assignment, I selected two short stories called 'War Games' and 'After the Cultural Revolution' (Students of Jarvis Collegiate 1983). These stories reflected situations similar to those discussed in our previous class, and I hoped that their representation in published text would inspire my students' writings.

The students were first asked to read the stories silently underlining any lexical or grammatical items unfamiliar to them. Next, a student read a short passage aloud, usually a paragraph or several sentences, after which I repeated the same passage correcting pronunciation difficulties that the student had. Then I asked if there were any words, phrases, or grammar forms that were unfamiliar. Some words were written on the board along with their variants (e.g., ideo'logy/ideolo'gical). This activity proceeded until the end of the stories.[1]

After finishing the stories, I asked several comprehension questions specific to events that occurred in the text. Next, I placed the students in groups of three or four to work on a group speaking exercise. Several open-ended questions were written on the board that drew upon personal experiences as well as analyses of different textual styles and their social uses.

(On the blackboard) Discuss these questions in your group:

1) What are the differences between these stories and news reports in a newspaper?
2) Why do children play war games?
3) Why do children think war is fun?
4) What are the most important ideas in these stories?

Teacher's Note: These questions, particularly #1, were intended to provide an alternative view to the depersonalized reporting of war typical in the news media. They also emphasized the connection of this lesson to Lesson #1 and the future goal of sharing their experiences with the children.

LESSON 3: Writing a short story or paragraph on any subject pertaining to our discussions on the Gulf War

Teacher's Note: Before the students began to write, I reviewed earlier exercises that explored writing mechanics, sociocultural expectations in writing, and contrastive rhetoric. Of the latter, the writings of Covey (1983) and Matalene (1985) have been particularly informative. The students had approximately thirty minutes to work on a draft for my review. During in-class writing, I went from student to student and helped with any problems that they had.

Some students felt uncomfortable with the assignment, so when the class time ended, I made the completion of the assignment optional.

Some compositions didn't turn up until a month later, some not at all. Again, the reasons are complex. For some the topic brings back too many painful memories. Others are uncomfortable writing because the high status conferred upon the written word in their L1 engenders feelings of inadequacy in L2 writing. Also, the culture of politics for many students has instilled a great hesitancy to commit ideas to script, particularly if they diverge from the status quo in any way. This has been expressed to me several times and I try to accommodate that sensitivity in my assignments.

Here is an example of a student's composition with some lexical and grammatical corrections included:

My Experience of War
During the T.V. news it was reported that the Gulf War was over. The program showed many joyful people celebrating very happily. When I watched the pictures, it brought back my memory. During the Second World War, many families were destroyed by the brutal war. Also, my family lost a lot of property but fortunately our people were all alive. Running away from the cruel enemy, we went to many large cities and small villages; finally we settled in Chongqing. I found a boarding school in the village. One day in 1945, I went back to the city and visited my parents and also celebrated the August Moon. After dinner I went out to buy some fruit. Suddenly, I saw a jeep full of air force men. They were very happy singing, laughing and hugging each other. The people were yelling loudly, 'The war is over! The war is over!' The next day I went back to school and told the good news to the principal and my schoolmates, but no one would believe me.

LESSON 4: Discussion between adult ESL class and Grade 7s
The class reviewed the questions and ideas from Lesson #1 before meeting with the Grade 7 students. Both classes met in the regular Grade 7 classroom. After introductions, the first student to speak was my student from Iran. She began to talk about how sad she felt about the war and how terrible it must be for the children. After only a few sentences, the Grade 7 teacher interrupted her

and asked, 'You don't want Saddam to rule the world, do you?' I was shocked but didn't say anything. To my pleasant surprise, my student refused to be intimidated. She continued to say that Saddam was a bad man but that war was not fair. The teacher countered by asking, 'What would you do if a robber came to your house, attacked your family, and stole your property? Would you do nothing? That's what Saddam did in Kuwait.' My student, of high-intermediate language skills, continued to speak her mind, and the sight of one's student forcefully debating a native speaker of English was very satisfying.

Another one of my students pointed to the classroom teacher and said, 'I completely agree with you.' I was surprised because he had not stated this view in our previous discussions. This was a moment to reflect on how my teaching practices might have silenced his point of view. Most of the discussion that followed was conducted between the classroom teacher and my students. If any of my students tried to personalize or depoliticize their experience of war, she interrupted. More than anything, I was graphically made aware that the most powerful and challenging political statements are not measured by content but by the specific time and situation of their expression. In this way, mundane events can become politically charged because they detract attention from the depiction of conflict as a necessary consequence of two competing ideologies – one good, the other evil. When my Vietnamese student talked about the bombing of Hanoi, the teacher asked, 'You came to Canada for freedom, right? To escape communism, right?' Unfortunately, none of the Grade 7 students spoke or asked questions.

When we were back in our classroom, I asked the students how they felt about the encounter. One student commented, 'We wanted to talk about our experience, but she kept stopping us.' To this, another student joked, 'Just like China. She has to keep to the official line.'

Initially, I found this to be a very depressing and wasteful experience. But after a while I realized that many positive things occurred. For the Grade 7s, it was probably their only opportunity to hear different perspectives, however harassed, about the nature of warfare. For these children, the existence and recognition of dissenting opinions is an essential prerequisite for developing new social possibilities if they so choose.

LESSON 5: *Globe and Mail* vocabulary and student writing (approximately two hours)

Teacher's Note: One day, the Globe and Mail *newspaper printed a collection of terms that had been used by the British press to describe the Gulf War (see Appendix 1). The article was called 'Jingoism: Mad Dogs and Englishmen.' The article displayed two parallel columns of similar terminology, but one representing 'us,' the coalition forces in the conflict, and the other representing 'them,' the Iraqis. Invariably, the connotations for 'us' were positive and for 'them' negative. Thus these parallel lists effectively demonstrated the fallacy of language neutrality. By saying one thing, while implicitly referring to another, words and texts are used to make insinuations that might otherwise transgress public credibility and legal norms (cf. Ricouer's notion of 'split referentiality' in Janks 1989).*

With this text, I wanted my students to be aware of some of the complex ways in which persuasion/coercion can be 'hidden' within the English language.

The students were given a copy of the article. First, I referred to the earlier lesson where we explored the differences between news reports and personal journals. Then I wrote the words 'jingoism' and 'patriotism' on the board. Students were asked what they knew about these two words, and we discussed their similarities and differences. I asked the students whether they thought patriotism was good or bad. Everyone said it was good for a nation, but too much patriotism was a problem. When I asked, 'How do you teach patriotism?' one student recalled a story from his youth in occupied Hong Kong: 'In Japan, the teacher gives a taste of the sweet fruit to the students and asks, "Do you like it? Do you want more? Take it from China."' Another student said, 'Patriotism is not bad; bad leaders use patriotism to cheat the people.'

I then wrote 'Only mad dogs and Englishmen stay out in the noon day sun,' on the blackboard to stimulate discussion and to draw a connection to the terms 'jingoism' and 'patriotism' on the blackboard. First, we discussed the discomfort of noon heat and then the incongruous image of the sun-burnt, 'mad' Englishmen. Then the conversation moved to the question of why the Englishman was in a country with such a hot sun. This drew references of personal experience of colonialism from my class. We discussed historical events from Hong Kong, Iran, and Belize where jingoism played a part in justifying foreign occupation.

On the blackboard, I drew a long horizontal line. On the left end I wrote 'neutral feelings/small reaction.' On the right end, I wrote 'strong feelings which cause a reaction.' On the left side I wrote, 'He is not the most popular person in the world,' in the middle, 'He is not popular,' and on the right end, 'People hate him.' I then suggested that a reporter would have a choice when describing an unpopular politician, and that rather than being neutral, the choice of words could cause different feelings in the reader and possibly persuade the reader to feel a certain way. An older student from the Philippines then said that when he was young, he had learnt about looking for the difference between the *appearance* and the *essence* of the text. I liked the concept, so I wrote the words on the board and asked the student to elaborate. I then wrote the assignment on the blackboard.

(On the blackboard) You are a reporter for the *London Times* or the *Baghdad Herald*. Describe a scene from the war or an interview with Bush or Saddam. Remember them/us vocabulary from the newspaper article.

Student example (Vocabulary from article underlined):

1) From Baghdad: Saddam Hussein is taking an act of great statesmanship by ordering his army to withdraw from Kuwait and end the war immediately. He wins the praise from all peace-loving people throughout the world.

2) From London: Saddam Hussein accepts defeat after suffering a high rate of attrition from allied bombing and shelling. His decision to withdraw from Kuwait before the coalition's main forces

arrive and have a hard fight is <u>blundering and cowardly</u>, but he said his army has finished the 'Holy War' duty.

LESSON 6: Exercise related to *Globe and Mail* article

Teacher's Note: Lesson 5 had posed some difficulties. Some students became overly focused on learning all the vocabulary instead of using selected items for the assignment. I developed an additional exercise (see Appendix 2) as a way to explore further the processes in which ideology and language intersect. I was particularly influenced by Althusser's concept of interpellation (Weedon 1987, 30–1). Interpellation is the manner in which language draws one into a prefigured and partial way of knowing the world. One's use of language then becomes a kind of filter, directing us to favour certain representations of the world over others. But this integration is hidden. As we use language we assume a complete mastery over our ideas instead of recognizing their source as 'outside' of our conscious experience – our 'subjectivity' (ibid) – and connected to structures of social power. I was fascinated with trying to present poststructural concepts in a format that was more easily accessible for my class.

I gave each student a copy of the assignment and asked them to read the top paragraph to themselves. I then asked them if there were any problems with the vocabulary, grammar, or ideas. Many of the students didn't understand my analogy. For starters, several women were not convinced of the inseparability of spices/meanings within. One suggested that a sugar cube could absorb certain flavors while another student's remedy was the addition of water. I decided to do the first couple of examples on the blackboard with the whole class.

For the category of meaning, I emphasized the literal use for the word. On the board we came up with the following material:

WORD	MEANING(S)	USES/CONTEXTS	FEELING +/-/n
Horde	a large group	a group of animals, locusts, ants, bees	- (negative)
Lads	young boys, men	boy scouts, military sports teams, school, discipline, training, cooperation, energy	+ (positive)

Teacher's Note: I asked a series of questions and wrote responses on the blackboard to emphasize the processes of connotation that occur in metaphor.

(For example #1)
Teacher: When you think of locusts, bees or ants, how do you feel?
Students: Afraid, scared, shaky, irritated.
Teacher: It's impossible to take these feelings away from the word. Now what do you think of a horde of shoppers, people, refugees, or children?
Students: (laughter)
One student: Can I say a horde of teachers?
Students: (more laughter)
Teacher: Sure.

The students then worked in groups of three to complete the exercise as we had done on the blackboard together. I went from group to group helping and discussing the various ideas. I made a point of emphasizing the difference in #4 between the verb and the more common adjective, *neutral*. One of my students best summed up the difference by saying that with the verb *neutralize*, 'Someone is interfering.'

For #7, the distinctions between the positive, negative, or neutral feelings of 'defiant' were debated. The students decided that context determined sentiment. One student said that if your children are defiant, then its a negative term. Another student, however, pointed out that if someone is fighting against bad laws, then defiant is a positive term.

Teacher's note: This was exactly what I wanted to accomplish, and I was pleased to see students think of language as contextual and tied to issues of power.[2] For myself, the most satisfying moment of the class was when one student said. 'So, journalists are not neutral.'

Several problems did occur with this exercise. Two students were unable to deal with the vocabulary in this meta-contextual format. They preferred to write sentences to elaborate or explore the meanings of the words. I realized, in retrospect, that the exercise did bias conceptual skills of an analytical type. Those students who could easily detach and categorize language items would find this exercise more useful than students more experienced in associative and holistic literacy skills.

Conclusions

As ESL teachers in our society, we hold limited faith in the rhetoric of idealism. Our world is most often focused on the short horizon, the measurably accomplished within finite parameters. The immeasurable has less value, so we rarely consider the motivational power of 'impractical' ideas. Perhaps it is time to reconsider our biases and our priorities. The boundaries upon inquiry are not divine acts but social constructions that have and will change. We can pretend that our place is to just impart the 'facts,' or we can educate for an active agency in the process of change.

Critical pedagogy makes no claims to improve the world singularly, but it refutes a notion of teaching as locked in time and fixed to the location of the classroom. 'When we teach,' according to Simon, 'we are always implicated in the construction of a horizon of possibility for ourselves, our students and our communities' (1992, 56). To this end, I have suggested that the educational possibilities of political discourse need to be explored and expanded in the ESL classroom. The pursuit of distant aspirations is a worthy educational focus. It can't be easily measured by aptitude tests, but it can inspire people towards achievements that are otherwise thought impossible.

My students and I shared an important educational experience. Its uniqueness was the unexpected convergences of our community setting, our histories, and the unplanned events that influence our lives. Discussing the Gulf War, I believe, did not come at the expense of more 'important' endeavours, but enhanced the acquisition and retention of the language skills that we hope to impart. Our classes were not without their moments of difficulty, but strategies to express and resolve diverse social ideas are essential learning activities in the class and the community. For the teacher, it may require valuing student participation over conformity to one's vision. This doesn't relegate the teacher to apolitical silence but to discretion: quite simply, it may mean discarding transitive statements such as 'I disagree with you,' in favour of reflections such as 'I have another idea.' With this type of strategy, I believe, we are more likely to identify and promote collective notions of social justice through our lessons.

Regardless of one's opinion on the Gulf War, it has set into motion many new realities that are frightening for the future. For the young, war has become a sanitized entertainment indistinguishable from a football game, cartoon show, or a video arcade. Contrary to 'New World Order' rhetoric, the ignorance of war's reality is a disturbing legacy for the future, in which a public desire to resolve dispute through aggression becomes, once again, the norm rather than the exception. Our legacy for future generations becomes even more disturbing when we consider the proliferation of ever more efficient means of technological destruction.

The narrowing of public debate has other frightening consequences. As my students' experiences have taught me, patriotism is often one of society's most privileged forms of amnesia. The euphoria of patriotic victory, with its intolerance for dissent, easily transfers to other areas of public debate. Those ascribed the status of dissenters then find themselves increasingly vulnerable. Such developments, if not challenged, engender the formation of totalitarian authority. Educating for a critical and active democracy, then, is not only about the present but about the future. And in many important ways, our ESL classes anticipate the type of diverse community we are becoming. Such opportunities are unique and worthy of our best energies.

CHAPTER 3

Critical Practice for a Changing World of Work

Introduction

Finding a job may be the most difficult task facing a newcomer to Canada. In this regard, the ESL classroom is an obvious place to teach specific skills for the immediate and pressing need to find employment. Often, this is a frustrating experience, as teachers evaluate the effectiveness of job-related language programs in a changing world of work that appears increasingly unstable and unpredictable. 'What should we teach? Is this material relevant for the jobs available to our students?' Such questions are particularly unsettling as many ESL teachers nervously assess their own employment prospects within the context of increasing pressures for budget constraints in education. As well, conflicting and often contradictory economic advice from 'experts' compounds the frustrations teachers feel when asked to provide students with suggestions for job-search strategies.

There is a tendency, encouraged by many policy makers, to think of our current economic difficulties as temporary, requiring only familiar monetary and educational policies to restore the prosperity and growth that have characterized Western economies since the Second World War. Others find such forecasts unrealistically optimistic. According to Richard Gwyn (*Toronto Star*, Sunday, 2 August, 1992, B3), low growth and increased job displacement represent a 'normal' state of affairs in this century. In his view, we are once again following an economic pattern in which we cannot assume continuous economic 'progress,' profitability from property investment, and the unqualified benefits of individual competitiveness.

But we should not be totally disheartened. As noted by Gwyn, perhaps the greatest difference between our current recession/depression and the 'hard times' of the early twentieth century is the relative security that we have now. It is important to remember, however, that this security was obtained through determined and often difficult political action, which culminated in the creation of our social welfare system. Furthermore, political activism was not the exclusive domain of respected and established families. Far from it. Then as now, those who advocated 'short-term pain for long-term gain' enjoyed considerable immunity from the immediate social consequences of their own prescriptions. Not surprisingly, they were also reluctant to consider any tinkering with the foundations of their privilege. It was this contentious environment that propelled much of the trade union movement in Canada and the farmer's cooperatives on the prairies. In many cases, immigrants were at the forefront of these struggles. After coming so far to begin a new life, many of them were unwilling to passively accept onerous conditions reminiscent of their native countries. Perhaps it was the experience and perspective of newcomers – an ability to see beyond the encumbrance of local history – that motivated their activism.

Certainly then, and especially now, new Canadians are aware that the world of work is not a given, 'natural' thing, but represents social decisions and frequently contested social choices. No one is better positioned to understand the decisions required to improve the possibilities for newcomers than newcomers themselves. Nevertheless, ESL teachers can provide critical insights and language skills that encourage our students in this process, as I suggest in this chapter. The following discussion and lessons are intended to show how a newspaper article was used for this purpose in our class.

Immigrants' Impact

In September, 1991, the *Toronto Star* ran a three-part series written by Paul Watson called 'Immigrants' Impact.' The first article in the series (Watson 1991, A1, A8) was selected to encourage students to think critically about the role of immigrants in Canada's changing economy. The title of the piece, 'Foreign-born workers keep Metro moving,' emphasized an evaluation of immigrant labour that, in the opinion of the paper, obviously needed reinforcing in the general Toronto community and would certainly be of interest to my students.

'New report explodes myths' was the caption above the title. The major 'myth' to which Watson directed his argument was that immigrants are an unnecessary burden upon the community. Particularly during times of economic recession, immigrants are vulnerable to both simplistic and sophisticated forms of public exclusion. According to Watson, 'Critics of Canada's immigration policy have long argued that its emphasis on reuniting families allows too many people without the right job skills to settle here. Their solution would be to cut back on family-class immigrants and select more independent workers with better education and training. Some go further and call for a cutback on immigration from Third World countries, assuming most of them are dirt poor and dumb' (Watson 1991, A8).

Using information from the Economic Council of Canada and Statistics Canada, Watson challenges these assumptions: 'The proportion of Third World immigrants with university degrees is still higher than in the Canadian-born population' (1991, A8). Furthermore, those who lack diplomas are most often doing jobs that native-born Canadians refuse to do. Watson went on to discredit several other similar 'myths.' He showed that, in comparison to native-born Canadians, immigrants are less likely to end up on welfare, more likely to end up in managerial positions, and have a slightly higher average income. Without immigrant labour, according to Watson, much of Toronto's economy would shut down. 'Immigrants' Impact' also gave a detailed breakdown of the percentage of foreign-born workers in a variety of sectors in the economy. This profile served to focus both on the possibilities and the limitations that immigrants faced in their search for employment.

Lesson Plans

In a program that has continuous intake or mixed proficiency levels, such as the advanced class that participated in these activities, a topic-based syllabus is an effective way to avoid many potential difficulties (see Nunan 1988). Relevant and interesting content allows the teacher to introduce and reinforce a variety of language skills with greater effectiveness. Also, individual needs can be addressed within the larger topic frame without submitting the entire class to redundant materials.

When I evaluate and select material like 'Immigrants' Impact' for my class, I also consider the article within the context of my students' expectations as second language learners: What kind of speaking, listening, reading, and writing activities can be incorporated in the topic over the course of a week or two? Which grammatical or functional structures can I introduce or review? What interesting idiomatic material is present in the text?

LESSON 1: Speaking activity to prepare students for ideas in 'Immigrants' Impact' article (approximately one hour)
The students were placed in groups of three to work together on the following questions written on the blackboard. These four questions were a direct adaptation from a 'myth/fact' abstract that was featured on the covering page of the article.

(On the blackboard)

1) Who do you think have a higher average income: foreign-born or Canadian-born workers? Why?
2) Who do you think are more likely to end up on welfare: immigrants or those born in Canada? Why?
3) Who do you think have a higher education: immigrants or Canadian-born? Why?

4) In your opinion, what kinds of jobs are most common for foreign-born workers in Canada: management positions or menial labour? Why?

Teacher's Note: Before the students began their group discussion, I clarified any difficulties with the questions on the board. In particular, a distinction between Canadian citizen *and* Canadian-born *was made: A Canadian citizen can also be an immigrant. The notion of* menial labour *was also discussed. Brief reference was made to language items that might be useful for this discussion, such as comparative and equative structures as well as opinion markers and polite forms of disagreement.*

After the discussion, I brought the whole class together to talk about each group's ideas. I did this by conducting a poll similar to the statistical material found in the 'myth/fact' abstract from the article. Regarding question #1, none of my students believed the article's 'fact' that foreign-born workers have a slightly higher income ($27,610 vs. $26,427). In #2, most of my class agreed with the 'fact' that immigrants are less likely to end up on welfare (3.5% vs. 5.5%). For question #3, a slight majority of the students agreed with the 'fact' that foreign-born adults are better educated (27.5% vs. 22.6% with university education). The obvious reason put forward by several students was the point system for immigration, which increases the chances for highly educated individuals. Finally, the 'fact' that foreign-born workers were proportionately higher represented in professional and managerial positions (question #4) was treated with a great deal of scepticism by my students. Several students with impressive managerial experience recounted personal stories of rejection for employment due to an absence of 'Canadian experience.'

LESSON 2: Reading of 'Immigrants Impact' (approximately two hours)
Because of the length of Watson's article, I had my students read only the first half, which contained a general discussion, rather than the latter half, which featured statistical analyses. The

students were, however, given copies of the charts of statistics, which indicated the numbers of immigrants in various employment sectors (mechanics; machinists and maintenance; food, hospitality, etc.; manufacturing and transportation; and so on). I numbered the paragraphs and asked the students to read the article quietly to themselves underlining any words, phrases, ideas, or grammar that they might not understand.

After the students completed their first reading, I reviewed the selection collectively with the class. First, a student would read a short passage, usually a paragraph or several sentences, after which I repeated the same passage correcting any difficulties that the student had. Then I asked students if there were any words, phrases, or grammar forms that were unfamiliar. Some words were written on the board with emphasis placed on their pronunciation. This format proceeded until the end of the stories.

Teacher's Note: Often, the response to my query about problems in textual comprehension is silence. I then select passages or words that I suspect are difficult for the students and ask them – no one in particular – for the meaning. Usually, the word that I select is not understood. I recognize that the initial silence reflects the embarrassment that some feel when they attract public attention upon a gap in comprehension.

This discomfort often leads to a dependence on dictionary use. Excessive dictionary use tends not only to isolate and distort meanings out of context, but it can also reflect a false sense that one's knowledge is uniquely inferior to other students'. I often discourage dictionary use by reminding students that if they don't know a word, the chances are excellent that other students feel the same way. Also, the oral negotiation of vocabulary items amongst peers serves as a challenging activity, particularly for those who have had more experience with written English, and highlights the inherent instability and dynamic nature of meaning in signifying systems.

After this review of the selection, I prepared a short vocabulary review and series of questions for a group-speaking activity. Several interesting idioms were used in this article. For example, Watson refers to immigrants as 'the backbone of the dry cleaning industry' (Watson 1991, A8). We discussed both the cultural component of the idiom – the choice of 'backbone' (rather than heart, for example) as the foundation of the body – and the metaphorical use of the word: the foundation of the industry. We then discussed the use of 'backbone' in a variety of other cultures: for example, an essential support for any undertaking.

I wrote three questions on the blackboard that were designed to encourage experiential relationships to the text.

1) Why was this story written?
2) Which occupations are the easiest/most difficult for immigrant workers to find? Why?
3) Can the government do anything to make certain jobs more accessible?

Teacher's Note: With a class of mixed ability, such 'open-ended' questions are important for encouraging participation. As well, this approach provided a refreshing departure from the previous activity where literacy skills were primarily focused upon comprehension of isolated words, phrases, and grammar forms. For an excellent discussion of levels of literacy, see Wells (1987). In particular, questions #1 and #3 are representative of Wells' notion of an epistemic level of literacy. Such questions reinforce the social potential of reading and writing to bring about change in individuals and subsequently in the greater community. They are designed as an engagement with texts that encourages 'creativity, exploration, and critical evaluation' (Wells 1987, 110–11).

For question #1, I mentioned adverbial clauses and phrases of purpose to assist in the discussion. Examples using 'so that/in order that/in order to' were briefly discussed.

In the group discussions, many interesting ideas and perspectives circulated. One student commented that a recession breeds intolerance. Another student referred to personal experience by reminding the class that established immigrants can also be intolerant to recent arrivals. One student discussed his personal frustration with employers who insisted upon Canadian experience. He pointed out that after the political change in Eastern

Europe, the potential for international trade was excellent and that no one could better negotiate the intricacies of doing work there than former residents. However, because my student received his engineering degree and experience working in Poland, Canadian professional associations and engineering companies were unwilling to recognize his experience and hire him. This student was quite bitter as he emphasized the link between Canada's sluggish economy and the lost potential for international trade that professional immigrants could provide.

LESSON 3: Writing assignment based on 'Immigrant's Impact' (approximately two hours)
I began the class by reviewing many of the comments made the previous day in Lesson 2. I then asked the class to write a short story on their impressions of the article. I referred to the post-reading questions from Lesson 2 as a possible guide. On the blackboard, I listed a few further suggestions:

1) Write about something that interests you.
2) Try not to make your topic too big.
3) Write down all your ideas in point form before you begin your story.
4) Remember grammar forms and idioms from the article.

Teacher's Note: The class had previously done exercises to increase their awareness of topic sentences, narrowing of topics, unity, and parallelism. Two resources that helped me in this regard were Bander (1980) and Dillon (1986).

I went from student to student, checking for any problems with the composition assignment. As always, some students followed my suggestions and others preferred their own approach, which is fine with me. A few students couldn't get started, so I would talk to them for a while and make a few suggestions. I reminded students to leave space between lines for the purpose of making corrections. I also emphasized that this was only a first draft and that I expected some changes to be made later.

LESSON 4: Peer reviews for student compositions (approximately one hour)
I began experimenting with peer reviews about two years ago. I see it as a wonderful opportunity for ESL students to experience how others comprehend their work, and, consequently, as a way to improve the communication of their ideas (see McGarrell 1992; Mittan 1989). One problem has always persisted in the peer review process, however, and that is the reluctance of many students to offer constructive criticism to each other. Certainly in many cultural experiences of learning, criticism is not valued, particularly from one's colleagues. Some students are doubtful of the ability of a peer to contribute to a composition. These are important points to consider. Nevertheless, I have found that the benefits compensate for the difficulties.

Because of the mixed abilities of my class, peer reviews can range from simple clarification of the words, structures, and intended meanings to complex debates over the merits of the ideas in the composition. Practical considerations tend to outweigh preferred pedagogical strategies. My preferred strategy is to pair people off with comparable ability, although this is sometimes difficult. Some students finish their work quickly, others go home to write major works, and a few never complete even a short paragraph. During the course of a peer-review session, I may have half the class still finishing their assignments and the other half in review pairs. I also try to have at least two people review each story, which can further complicate things.

Each member of a review pair is given a paper to fill out and return to the writer. The following questions are on the review paper:

1) In your opinion, what were the main ideas in this text?
2) What ideas did you find the most interesting?
3) Which ideas/sections are not clear to you?

After the peer reviews, I asked the class to look over their papers and make any changes that they felt necessary. Then I asked them to submit their 'finished' version to me for further comments and corrections. Once again, this process can range over several days due to the varied degrees of completion of the assignment.

Teacher's Note: After several stories are corrected, I read them out loud to the students at the beginning of the next day's class. I may repeat a story several times and write vocabulary items on the board or point out good use of structural and idiomatic material that we had reviewed. Also, I will ask students for general comments or comparisons of the experiences or the ideas in the different compositions. This activity has several linguistic and social benefits. Developing the ability to comprehend and paraphrase larger passages is a useful listening activity, although the stylistic differences between written and spoken language make this somewhat artificial. But the boost to self-confidence may outweigh this disadvantage. Some students feel that their work is not good enough to share with others. The teacher's presentation, in this regard, enhances the legitimacy of the student's text and the value of the author's ideas by making them the focus of classroom time. A native speaker's enunciation of a corrected work, I believe, further encourages confidence in a second language writer.

Student Compositions

The following are examples of student compositions from the assignment. Some lexical and grammatical corrections have been included by student request. Some students wrote titles for their work.

This story was written in order to make Canadians accept foreign-born people. When they come to Canada, immigrants don't only accept welfare and cause increases in crime. They can also help Canadians propel economic development.

The government should make more programs to help immigrants with job-search skills and speaking skills. When a newcomer first looks for work, communication is the biggest problem. Canadian work experience is also a problem. Even if you have a lot of experience in your country, it is no use in Canada if you don't have a Canadian certificate. Employers never hire a person who doesn't have Canadian experience for a high position. So, they only work in lower positions.

To Quan

I think the 'Immigrants' Impact' article was written for native-born workers and for foreign-born workers as well. The idea of this story is to show them and to make them aware of the immigrants' power in Canada (or in Toronto). It was directed to the native-born workers in order to show them that the immigrant work force is very important to the city of Toronto, and it was directed to the foreign-born workers to show them that they have an important role in this city so that they can build their self-esteem against the immigrant myths. Also, they stay aware of the best and the worst positions they can occupy.

In my opinion the government could help the immigrants by giving them more confidence, simplifying the bureaucracy (i.e., the forms to fill in), and trusting more in their capacity for work, so that the immigrants could have more opportunities to find jobs. I myself haven't looked for work yet because I can't go out to work while my baby is not in school. But, I am aware of the immigrants' difficulties in finding a job.

There was something in the story that really surprised me about the statistics. It was about the architects. For me it's really a surprise that 47% of architects are born outside of Canada, because the Canadian architecture is so modern and beautiful. I thought it was a Canadian 'merit.'

Celia

It Comes in Time

The article that was entitled 'Immigrants' Impact' is a wonderful work. It comes at the best timing. Since we have an economic recession, many people are unemployed and on welfare. Some of them don't understand why there is a recession and they can't find an answer. They believe, therefore, that immigrants are the cause of their unemployment, and they are also their competitors in the labour market. So, they hate them although they have done a great deal of good work for the nation.

The purpose of this article is to make Canadians understand that immigrants are not a liability but an asset to Canada. In order to develop Canada more effectively and create more jobs for people, more immigrants in fact are needed. The evidence of this conclusion is in the accompanying list of the report.

At last, I was very surprised after reading this enlightening article on the statistics that were so good and detailed as to conjure up the image of hardworking and resourceful immigrants in the construction of Canada. I hope, from now on the native Canadian will have a better relationship with the immigrants.

Max

Immigrants Help Canada

I think many native-born people are always writing letters to the newspaper and complaining that the government allows too many immigrants to come into Canada. For this reason, the *Toronto Star* wrote the story with figures to prove that newcomers are useful for this country.

Recently, I have read a story in a Chinese newspaper about Vancouver's native-born people hating newcomers and being jealous of them. I think the Canadian-born people didn't understand the situation. In fact, many immigrants bring a lot of money, manpower, and skills when they come to Canada, and they help propel the Canadian economy into the future.

Everybody knows that the Canadian people are getting older, and the population would go without the new immigrants who pay the taxes and who support the seniors. So, the conclusion is the government should plan their immigration policy each year to accept as many newcomers as we need to maintain the country's prosperity.

Kam

In my opinion this story wanted to give us some information about how Canada's foreign-born and native-born people can manage in many difficult kinds of jobs and how they are the backbone of Canada's economy.

Now we are aware of this matter. As a result, we can tolerate each other much better than before and have deep cooperation with each other. Therefore, we can make a better future and also help to develop the country. Besides, the story provides an opportunity for people to live with each other in respect and friendship. As a consequence of this story, we understand now that immigrants are the backbone of Canada's survival, and it is an advantage for both native- and foreign-born people.

Mahin

Immigrants? Canadians?

'Why do we have to pay the immigrants?'

'Why do I have to line up here? Those immigrants!'

We can hear these words everywhere: on streets, in civic offices, on subways. Immigrants are blamed for being a burden on Canada. The Canadian government supposedly spends a lot of money on social welfare and education. In addition, people believe that the high crime rate is attributed to Asian immigrants. Immigrants make the social order worse and bring a lot of problems to Canada.

To a certain extent, it seems immigrants are an encumbrance to Canada and their contributions sink into oblivion. In fact, they are vital to the nation. Since the last two decades, there have been many people coming to Canada. They leave their home countries to seek a better life. Many of them come here with special training and experience in particular fields. They participate in the workforce and contribute to the industry and business of Canada. This makes Canada stay competitive with the other developed countries in the market. Moreover, they move to Canada and make Canada their permanent home. They don't want to see Canada being ruined. Indeed, they want Canada to be an Eden for themselves.

On the other hand, people have to bear in mind that the original people of North America are nobody but Indians and Inuits. All the rest are immigrants or descendents of immigrants. If Asian people had arrived here earlier, they would have called the others immigrants or descendents of immigrants. Now, even those Asian people who have lived here for generations are still labelled as immigrants in terms of their faces and skin colours. If everybody could remove the boundary between human beings, they would live more happily. We hope everybody in Canada has a heart of gold and helps to build a country for all people.

Marina

These stories offer many useful insights for ESL instructors. At the level of lexical and grammatical acquisition, it's interesting to note the incorporation of items from Watson's article. At another level, Wells' epistemic level, learners may be practising more important skills. Clearly, these writers most appreciated the status and legitimacy that immigrant labour received in this article. Their experiences, which informed their unique reading of the text, revealed an understanding of the world of work from which we, as ESL instructors, can learn. That is, the authors portray a world of work that is inextricable from issues of social power and social exclusion. These issues may involve the simplistic and overt forms of racism common during economic crises. Or, as some of the compositions note, immigrants may also be victimized by systemic forms of discrimination that exist between the rhetoric and the reality of our legal and social institutions.

What challenges does this pose for the ESL classroom? An emphasis on work-related strategies to the exclusion of the 'larger' picture is somewhat patronizing. Students are acutely aware of the contradictions in their situation. Many of them have been selected for citizenship by our government for their exemplary skills and education. Yet when they apply for the very jobs for which they are trained, they are told that they require 'Canadian experience' or 'Canadian accreditation' – a somewhat sophisticated form of discrimination that bureaucratically protects the perpetrator. Not surprisingly, those elite occupations with the greatest social power are able to perpetuate the myth that their 'special' training could not possibly be duplicated in a developing country.

Language is central to this equation, for it is in language that forms of discrimination that escape legal reprimand are encoded. Moreover, it is through language that students might get the results they need from reluctant individuals and institutions. The practical challenge for ESL teachers is to explore the culture of authority in which we reside and to help our students with the language skills necessary to participate and act in their best interests.

Exploring Public Language / Cultural Authority

Through my students' experiences, I've come to appreciate the great extent to which work is uniquely practiced, evaluated and rewarded in our society. When we 'get ahead' or 'play the game' we are indeed relying upon an inventory of culturally acquired language skills. Furthermore, these learned qualities, which we often take for granted, are balanced precariously on a shifting sociolinguistic fence. Take, for instance, the fine line that separates the public perception of confidence versus arrogance, or honesty versus indiscretion. The issue, from the perspective of an ESL teacher, is not so much to say which is wrong and which is right but to examine the social contexts in which specific language options are used, and to explore how and why such options command respect, engender confidence, or result in silence.

What I suggest here is an area of inquiry that requires a genuine dialogue with our students – not only to learn about them, but also to learn about ourselves. In Roger Simon's words, it means exploring ways of teaching that will 'simultaneously organize and disorganize a variety of understandings of our natural and social world' (1992, 56). It is an area of inquiry in which critical pedagogy can make an important contribution to ESL and ESL work curricula.

In *Learning Work*, Simon, Dippo, and Schenke (1991) emphasize the importance of using students' experiences to examine work critically. They describe two complementary approaches: *working on* and *working with* experience. *Working on* experience can be simply described as 'taking apart' personal experiences, or distancing oneself from the things that are taken for granted. In regards to work, this means learning how one's common-sense understanding of work has been formed by social and historical processes. Appropriate pay, conduct between employers and employees, or what constitutes a safe work place would be examples. An individual worker would have 'internalized' a sense of right and wrong pertaining to the responsibilities and benefits from existing conditions of employment. *Working with* experience emphasizes comparison, drawing out similarities and differences within a group of students. This collective focus on experience further clarifies that 'common-sense' assumptions around work often reflect political decisions and impositions that can privilege particular social interests to the detriment of others. Gaining this knowledge, that common-sense assumptions are socially produced – and need not remain 'common,' but can be challenged – is an important tactic for public life.

For example, many of us share an assumption that 'competition' implies a set of rules to which all 'competitors' must adhere. Through *working with* ESL students' experiences, however, we discover that workers in some other countries must follow a different set of rules regarding the freedom to organize trade unions, change jobs, or ensure that equal standards of job safety and environmental protection be followed. Although we are frequently told in Canada that it is *our* productive behaviour that must be modified in order to 'compete' globally, in fact it is no longer a competition based upon equity or fairness, as promoted and assumed by the language that has framed the discussion. So when a local community is called upon to make unquestioning sacrifices in obedience to a putative economic 'fact,' such as 'competitiveness,' members of that community can potentially gain the confidence to insist that all possibilities must be carefully and publicly examined first.[1] They might insist, for example, that the rules of competition be the same for all participants – that foreign workers be allowed to compete equally with Canadians as *consumers*, not just producers. More importantly, as a precondition for equal competition, local workers could insist that foreign workers be allowed to participate safely in the decisions that define their working conditions and living environment. Such public advocacy and local initiative could result from working with experience and examining the uses of public language.

Critically examining our experiences of work helps learners 'increase their effective participation' in the decisions which determine their working lives (Simon, Dippo, and Schenke 1991, 11). Here is an example that occurred in our ESL classroom and specifically examined the issue of language. One day, our class discussed a situation in which one of the students had asked me to explain the meaning of a document received from her child's school. I had told her that I didn't fully understand the document because it was written in a language – a legal language – of which I wasn't sure. I suggested that she contact the principal of the school. In fact, the issue was more complex than simply decoding a text. I realize, in retrospect, that my hesitation also reflected the high social status placed on a legal document and my possible liability for advising my student to sign one. Fortunately, I also had a lawyer from Chile in my class. She added pertinent insights to the manner in which legal language communicates a wide range of meanings including privilege and *scarcity*, the economic creed where one's social and financial position grows exponentially to the restrictions placed on the skills which define it. My students realized that they need not feel inadequate if they don't understand something because language may be designed to be exclusive rather than inclusive; that is, to evade understanding and scrutiny rather than promote mutual comprehension. The students, *working with* their experiences, then looked at similar contexts of language use in their own native countries. As well, my students' insights gave me new perspectives with which to examine similar language practices in my own profession.

ESL teachers, like lawyers, participate in a world of work where specific sets of language and knowledge forms are linked to cultural forms of authority. That is, we learn how to construct what is conventionally held to be 'true' and of value within our occupation and within our society. Similar to lawyers, we can say one thing while doing several things at the same time. We can talk about new insights we have found while using language in a way that claims a certain stature and exclusivity within the profession that translates into high positions and salaries. A good part of this skill is learned on the job and enables us to survive if not progress in our work environment. It is 'insider' knowledge (Simon, Dippo, and Schenke 1991, 34–8) rather than the 'explicit' curricula studied in formal institutions, which comes from books and lectures on ESL or applied linguistics. And because 'insider' knowledge is rarely formalized, we often perceive it as something people have to 'figure out for themselves.'

Insider knowledge means gaining a sense or an implicit under-standing of hierarchies within a profession and the 'little things' that are required to get a job and then move up in status, power, and income. For example, in ESL and applied linguistics, publish-ing articles and making presentations at conferences are key to becoming professors, program coordinators, lead instructors, or curriculum consultants. To this end, aspiring individuals cultivate a specific language form or genre of writing and speaking (see Lakoff 1990, ch. 8). They strategically cite and quote 'authorities,' invoke the 'latest' research, and refer to 'findings' from their data to suggest some new truth has been 'discovered.' Insider knowl-edge, in this regard, means the careful management of appear-ances: using language forms that detach outcomes from deter-ministic research models; 'piggy-backing' controversial ideas onto the opinions of recognized experts; 'hiding' inconsistencies and speculations; 'borrowing' ideas from others in ways that elude lo-cal standards of plagiarism. Moreover, these 'appearances' can be used as weapons. At contentious staff meetings, when difficult de-cisions about space, funding, assessment, standards, and language curricula are being debated, the 'latest' research can be used by initiates to silence the opinions of uninitiated colleagues. Such knowledge forms are rarely discussed or acknowledged in formal settings, but I would argue that they are not an insignificant aspect of ESL or any other work environment. Insider knowledge is often what gets jobs and promotions, or forms networks that provide security in precarious work hierarchies.

As ESL professionals, our success in 'communicating' to an ex-clusive group of peers, and marking ourselves apart from others, provides the basis for our claims to higher position and salary in our competitive society. Acknowledging our exclusivity is not intended to diminish what we do. This acknowledgment is an 'experience' that we, as ESL teachers, can *work with* to understand learners' needs better when we teach work-related skills. We may need to examine both the explicit and implicit language skills – the 'little things' – that are necessary to work successfully in our society. As for the latter, we should remember that implicit knowledge is often misunderstood as 'cultural' knowledge – something with which we are born and which we acquire naturally, without conscious effort.[2] And to the detriment of our students, we may assume that such insider knowledge forms are outside the scope of ESL work curricula ('Students have to figure it out for themselves'). Through 'dialogue' with our students, such assumptions can be discovered and then challenged. Much of the follow-up to the 'Immigrants' Impact' lessons was faithful to this idea, as described below.

Beyond the Classroom

On 29 November 1991, the Toronto Association of Neighbourhood Settlement Houses sponsored a popular education forum called 'In the Picture.' Community centres throughout Toronto were asked to provide examples of how federal policies affected the daily lives of their clients. With the permission of my class, I gave the organization a copy of our 'Immigrants' Impact' compositions. At the event, several groups spoke to the assembly. One of my students, Celia, read her article, and I briefly spoke about what we had done in our class. Afterwards, the assembly broke into small discussion groups that focused on issues such as refugee/immigrant rights, public housing, and equity in the workplace. As well, each group had a facilitator who set out possible avenues of consultation and advocacy that linked grass-roots community organizations to various levels of government. The mix of immigrants and refugees with native-born Canadians at this event provided an invaluable opportunity for my students to witness firsthand an important aspect of our political culture.

One positive development is worth noting. Celia had had difficulties getting a daycare placement for her young son. She had been arbitrarily placed at the bottom of a waiting list because of an error about her status at the time of registration. Initially, the official in charge was reluctant to alter her decision. Finally, Celia personally went to the office and insisted that she be treated fairly. Her persistence paid off, and she obtained daycare and an opportunity to get a job. Taking this specific action, according to Celia, was a new experience for her. In her native Brazil, you couldn't accomplish the same results in this manner. In Toronto, however, with the encouragement from her local daycare worker, she succeeded. Her ESL classes also played a part. Celia noted that her initial expectation of learning English was a steady stream of grammar lessons. Instead, she found that our critical focus on relevant social issues provided her with a better perspective to participate effectively in community life.

On 23 May 1992, Marina and Max presented their compositions and ideas at a conference called 'Social Issues/Social Change and the ESL Classroom,' held at St. Stephen's Community House in Toronto. Their 'learners' panel' attracted an audience of teachers and administrators from various institutions in Ontario. Many important issues were discussed. Marina talked about her concern that certain ESL programs were too generally focused for students looking specifically for employment. In reply, one teacher noted that Marina could find more job-specific programs in the city. The group then shifted their discussion to an important debate about the merits of the existing evaluation of professional and educational qualifications of newcomers to Canada. For those satisfied with the status quo, it was a unique occasion to hear alternative views from colleagues. For those opposed, it provided evidence of the work yet to be done. For Max and Marina, it was an opportunity to participate in the process of negotiation/persuasion that characterizes the administrative development of policy in our community.

As mentioned earlier, the publishing and circulation of student compositions exposes students to a process of social and professional advancement familiar to educators in our society. For two years (1990–91, 1991–92), my advanced class at St. Stephen's Community House produced a book of student compositions entitled *Stories from Our Class*. Copies of the book are available at ESL resource centres, as well as the Modern Language Centre's library at the Ontario Institute for Studies in Education. Copies were also sent to the Ministry of Citizenship for their perusal. Several of my colleagues have used stories from the book for their classes. As well, I have presented chapters of the books at various conferences in Canada and abroad. The stories on 'Immigrants' Impact' feature prominently as the opening chapter of the 1991–92 edition (see Morgan 1992).

Marina assisted in many aspects of the book's production that year. Other students, particularly from the year before, actively took part in decisions about topics and design. Significantly, after the public success of the first edition, returning students wrote longer and more often. One of the most frequent comments from my students has been on the professional qualities of the copies. This should not be underestimated for its importance in motivating students or enhancing the public reception of their work. With current computer and laser publishing facilities, it is possible to produce materials independently that rival the quality of commercial publishing houses, at a minimal cost.

I see many benefits from this project. I've been able to work with learners on individual language problems, and I've been able to encourage my students to see themselves as writers, and possibly 'experts' in recognizing how public policy affects their lives in Canada.

Conclusions

'Immigrants' Impact' is an article situated in time and place. It conforms to the political culture in which we live and mobilizes a particular set of language resources with which certain social aims may be achieved. Its 'persuasiveness' – constructed through a careful use of structure, vocabulary, and statistics – reflects a society in which political power often requires negotiation, a degree of public consent, and justification in order to proceed as policy. Public policy on immigration or employment issues, then, is not just an act of fate, or the inexorable will of powerful social interests. Policy is often a compromise reflecting hard-fought concessions won by organized and informed citizens from all walks of life.

As in the past, newcomers need to learn the language skills necessary to get and do the jobs. But I believe newcomers should also be aware of the 'bigger picture' and the possibilities to transform the conditions of work that currently exist. This suggests a far 'closer' reading of the language of work as well as the public language that precedes policies on work (see Cooke's 'Model of Increasing Potential,' 1993, 92). What is the 'hidden agenda?' Whose interests are implicit in the language used to frame the discussion? What are the possibilities and language resources needed to challenge or modify the agenda? What kinds of 'insider' skills are necessary to participate effectively? Such concerns are language concerns and should be included in any ESL work curricula.

More than anything, the lessons and ideas in this chapter emphasize that work education in an ESL classroom is a collaboration between teachers and students. From students, teachers can better understand the contradictions and barriers that inhibit our students' participation in the workplace. In this way, teachers can make relevant changes in the way we teach and explore possibilities for extending our lessons beyond the confines of the classroom. Certainly, opportunities for change are abundant and close to home. Many of our ESL programs claim to 'empower' their students while rarely, if ever, consulting them in the hiring of teachers, the development of curricula, administrative policies, or decisions pertaining to educational budgets. Of course, such experiences are crucial and practical for successful entry into certain parts of our labour market. But perhaps more importantly, ESL students could address these issues in ways that better serve their own needs.

From teachers, students can learn how the gap between rhetoric and reality is often sustained through language and, sometimes, challenged through language. As Cummins says, 'critical thinking skills can be developed in students only by teachers who are themselves critical thinkers' (Cummins 1989b, 30). By exploring the contradictions in our own work environment, ESL teachers might better come to grips with the real barriers to employment that students encounter.

CHAPTER 4

Linking Dynamic Processes: Research, Identity, and Intonation

Teacher as Researcher

This chapter reflects upon what I judge to have been a particularly successful language lesson. What stands out most in this activity is how the foregrounding of social power and identity issues seemed to facilitate greater comprehension of sentence-level stress and intonation as strategic resources for (re)defining social relationships. Through reflection and theorizing, I hope to offer some insight on the weave of intended and unintended factors that determined the success of this lesson and make it important within the larger context of this book. First and foremost, the title and content of this chapter re-emphasize that critical practice and community development are not separate or inconsequential subjects reserved for the end of the day; they are applicable throughout the ESL curriculum, including lessons on grammar and pronunciation. In fact, as I will demonstrate in this chapter, issues of empowerment may be essential in terms of providing meaningful contexts for particular language activities. Second, the notion of a 'weave' applies as well to another major concern of this chapter: the ongoing exchange between theory and practice that informs my approach. Much of what happened in the class happened by chance, but more importantly, by a willingness to explore new ideas, both in terms of theory and pedagogy, in response to the particular experiences of my students.

Not long ago, a chapter such as this would be considered outside the realm of theory. At best, I could say that I was reflecting on the particular conditions of my *practice* – but not really theorizing. Formulating theory would require a certain degree of compliance with established scientific procedures: predetermined research objectives, systematic collection of data from a wide range of sources, rigorous techniques of evaluation, and ultimately a set of generalized and decontextualized conclusions that would be pertinent to the teaching of language anywhere and anytime – serious stuff best left to the experts at the university. The boundary between theory and practice has become increasingly blurred, however. It is now acceptable to speak of theorizing as a contingent or 'situated' activity; that is, concepts or even 'intuitions' generated from the unique circumstances that characterize each ESL classroom (see Canagarajah 1993, 1996; van Lier 1994). Moreover, the arbitrary separation of those who theorize and those who teach is being increasingly challenged. This new spirit is exemplified in Nunan's suggestion that 'teachers need to be able to conceptualise their practice in theoretical terms' (1990, 62). Nunan's advice is both appropriate and timely. It comes in response to the limited effectiveness of top-down curricula and the often exaggerated claims made in support of an ever proliferating body of theory and methodology (see Pennycook 1989; Dufficy 1993). Classroom teachers often find these materials 'too rigid' or 'too general' for their specific needs and subsequently feel justified in asking, 'Why not me? Why can't I develop my own theory for my own circumstances?' Why not, indeed.

In principle, I am in agreement with the call for more 'action,' 'qualitative,' and 'ethnographic' research approaches in ESL (see Cumming 1994; Nunan and Richards 1990).[1] Such teacher-directed inquiry would encourage greater flexibility and responsiveness to the diverse learning styles and experiences of students. At the same time, my enthusiasm is restrained by what I see as a lingering element of prescriptivism by some who currently advocate for more teacher-directed inquiry. It would not surprise me to see the second language field inundated with strict teaching manuals on *how* to theorize – a potentially self-defeating proposition. Such developments have little to do with innovations in research, as they represent a reluctance of established theoreticians to part with the prestige, career advancement, and remuneration associated with the 'ownership' of 'cutting-edge' ideas as they are promoted in published form. If such developments predominate, 'action' research may become more of a change in fashion rather than substance.[2]

It is important to consider that whatever claims to knowledge made on behalf of classroom research or ethnography in ESL come at a time when the discipline that invented many of its terms of reference, anthropology, is rethinking the fundamental purposes of this type of activity. Authors such as Clifford (1988) and Geertz (1983) often portray the ethnographic encounter as fundamentally interpretive, a form of self-fashioning that must be measured against the historical and cultural development of Western society, which has equated scientific methods with truth and has often sought out verification of its perceived superiority through its research imperatives (see Kuper 1973; Said 1978).

Educational ethnographers such as Erickson (1986) suggest that it is only through a process of *triangulation*, comparing observable phenomena with personal interviews and written documents, that we might possibly gain adequate understanding for our practice. Erickson also cautions that when conducting personal interviews, researchers should consider that some meanings and phenomena of social life are so 'common' to participants that they elude conscious understanding. Such meanings may be inaccessible to the researcher although they constitute ideological forms that are key to the ways that people understand and respond to their social world. Another factor, which is often downplayed, is that the classroom observer is actually observing the *effects* of his or her presence and status. Classroom researchers often believe that they can account for this situation by careful scrutiny of their own research biases. What are less clear, however, are the meanings that sustained observation and documentation evoke in ESL students, many of whom come from societies where classroom research methods can inadvertently parallel forms of political surveillance.

Let me elaborate. In my classes, I have often witnessed nervous students revise or 'forget' an unguarded comment in the face of my curiosity. Some have told me of their uncertainty regarding the permanence of their legal status, especially if they transgress public ordinances and relatively insignificant laws (e.g., jaywalking, undeclared tips on taxes). Others have mentioned their fears of retribution against family and friends back home as a result of a politically sensitive comment. And others, showing a critical awareness born of experience, have been suspicious of the fundamental assumptions that motivate inquiry.[3] In fact, just proposing a research study can be hazardous: students who are uneasy might be reluctant to say so in front of peers; consequently, they drop out of class without discussing their concerns.

Such experiences are carefully guarded and rarely discarded at the door of the classroom. What they suggest is that teachers who choose not to interview, tape record, or ask 'probing' questions should not be excluded from contributing to the knowledge base of our profession. This option becomes even more imperative when we consider the implications of identity work that explores language resources – such as intonation – to challenge power relations in the family, community and society. We might instead encourage teacher/researchers to 'discover' the ethical and ideological conditions in which freedom from observation and documentation becomes a necessary prerequisite for transformative practice. Based on such concerns, I have used few if any sources of empirical data (e.g., tape recordings, interviews, observations of other classes) in this chapter. Data collection took place over two days and consists almost exclusively of participant observation notes written immediately after our lessons from memory and from short phrases jotted down in class. Included as well are two examples of student compositions given to me with permission subsequent to my request.

Although I have initially diverged somewhat from the topic of intonation and identity, I hope to demonstrate that it is often through 'unconventional' associations and approaches that empowering language-learning environments are discovered and encouraged. As teacher researchers, we should always remember that the *boundaries* on the types of questions we ask, and the reasons for asking them, will most certainly direct the types of answers we 'find' and the social purposes to which we direct our findings.

Teaching Intonation in Context

The focus on the individual articulation and production of phonemes – meaningful contrastive sounds (segmentals) – was once the primary focus of pronunciation activities in ESL. As noted by Morley (1991), with the movement towards more communicative, functional-notional and task-based approaches, this emphasis seemed increasingly dated and out of place. There has been renewed interest and calls for greater awareness and integration of pronunciation activities throughout the ESL syllabus (Morley 1991; Murphy 1991). Attention to larger, sentence-level aspects of speech, such as in stress, rhythm, and intonation – collectively termed prosody or suprasegmentals – and various combinations of sounds, such as in linking, palatalization, assimilation, and reductions, are now more commonly featured along with suggestions for communicative approaches in pronunciation texts (see Avery and Ehrlich 1992; Beisbeir 1995; Gilbert 1993; Naiman 1992).

According to Crystal (1987, 169–71), the linguistic use of pitch, or melody – the intonation system – provides the most important suprasegmental effects in language. The use of rising or falling pitch contours (tones), or their combination, can serve a number of functions in an utterance. Intonation can effectively mark out clausal and sentence units, as well as provide coherence within and between larger informational units (e.g., the shift from one news item to another on a radio broadcast; Crystal 1997, 169–71).

Intonation can have other grammatical functions as well. Pitch contours can mark an utterance in the declarative mood ('You paid the bill') as either a statement (falling tone) or a question (rising tone). Also, pitch and stress together can provide *focus*, contrasting a specific lexical item with one that might occur in the same place with the same function (i.e., 'paradigmatic focus' in Kreidler

1989, 163). For example, focus placed on 'you' – with a specific tone (slow rising) – in the example above could be used to emphasize both displeasure and surprise within the general function of a question ('*I* should have paid the bill'). Focus can also be used to delineate the importance of information relative to what comes before and what comes after in an utterance (i.e., 'syntagmatic focus' in Kreidler 1989, 165). Such functions of intonation can be taught communicatively and integrated into various situational activities. Gilbert (1993) and Beisbeir (1995) offer many useful classroom exercises that demonstrate the various grammatical and semantic functions available through intonation and stress.

One particular function of intonation, in my experience, is not so easily taught in a controlled and analytical approach because the moment of its application is largely unpredictable and highly dependent on shifting meanings and intentions that reflect context and the perception of social relationships. Halliday (1985) describes this particular feature in his section entitled 'The dynamics of intonation': 'Once conversation starts, a new element is added: each new step defines the environment afresh' (58–60).

Several prosodic elements that enable this semantic movement are elaborated upon by Halliday and require a brief note here. The first important element is the vocal production of informational units, or *tone groups*, which provide the function of *tonality* (Halliday 1985, 54). Tonality thus sets up particular focal points to be more easily defined within an utterance. The boundaries of tone groups are not arbitrary, but rather reflect the informational intent of the speaker. Kreidler provides a good example (slanted lines indicate tone group markers): '(1a) /We don't want any/ (1b) /We/don't/want/any/' (Kreidler 1989, 156) In 1b, the speaker has probably used separate breaths and equal stress on each word to emphasize displeasure or irritation.

The second element of importance involves the establishment of specific focal points of prominence within tone groups. This function, which Halliday calls *tonicity*, is realized through the selection of a particular melodic contour, or *tone* (1985, 53); a speaker may select from a number of falling or rising tones, use them in combination, and vary their rate of inclination or declination in order to produce certain meanings. The match between a particular tone and its semantic function is never absolute, however; larger contextual and discursive elements can effect a speaker's actualization of tonicity. Of related interest, Crystal (1987, 171) distinguishes seven different tones and their functions for saying the word 'No!' Through elements such as tonality and tonicity, speakers respond to and define an interaction as it is being shaped and negotiated. With these elements, a speaker 'can indicate which are the content-bearing elements, vary the density with which new information is introduced, show how it relates to what has gone before, give it a particular "key signature" to indicate its relevance to this particular point – and direct the listener exactly to what he wants him to attend to' (Halliday 1985, 58–60).

The dynamics of intonation as described in Halliday's work would appear quite challenging to teach in an ESL classroom. One possible means of presentation would be analyses of various dialogues that could be transcribed and practiced by students. This would be beneficial, but it would diminish the use of intonation as a rhetorical device to reset priorities in response to largely emergent and unpredictable developments in a dialogue. Another useful approach would be to recognize 'unpredictability' as only a partial element of what was taking place in the dialogue. This concept of dialogue might be thought of as an ongoing *text*, a series of linguistic choices within various constraints or conventions of the *context of situation* (Halliday and Hasan 1985) in which it was unfolding, emphasizing the relative social positions of the discourse partners (its tenor), the social purpose and location of the dialogue (its field), and the specific function that language is supposed to achieve in the interaction and the linguistic elements used to realize it (its mode). This configuration of tenor, field, and mode would constitute what Halliday calls *register* (Halliday and Hasan 1985).

Halliday's social-semiotic approach to language, I believe, offers a potentially useful way to think about teaching intonation. Intonation is essential for the meaning potential of a spoken text; the meaning of a text cannot be understood separate from the specific context of its creation or expression. In the classroom, much

more attention and elaboration could be placed on *social* roles
when students participate in 'role play' exercises. The notion of
register might be useful for elaboration. When students ask, 'What
does intonation mean here?' they would be encouraged to ask as
well, 'Who is speaking? Why are they having this conversation?
What do they want to do with language in this situation?'[4] This
pedagogical approach would require establishing social contexts
that were relevant to students as a condition for developing the
prosodic and paralinguistic resources that are available to speakers in a given time and place. Furthermore, to better develop
awareness of the dynamic potential of intonation, teachers might
want to foreground contexts where the roles, responsibilities, and
privileges of social identity would be subject to (re)evaluation
in the context of new immigrant experiences. Finally, whenever
we talk of dynamics or change in social relationships, we are
invariably talking about power relations and the multiple ways
in which tradition, moral regulation, and authority are invoked,
modified, or resisted through language practices. So, ultimately,
ESL teachers would need to conceive of their students as having
social needs and aspirations that may be inseparable from linguistic needs if language instruction is to be most effective.

Social Identity in Transition

The students that participated in these lessons are all of Chinese
ethnicity. With the exception of one student from Malaysia and
one from Taiwan, the rest of the class comes from Hong Kong.
Of the fifteen students who participated in this class, eleven were
women and twelve were over the age of fifty. On the surface, a
great deal of homogeneity might be presumed. For the reasons
that I shall point out, however, and particularly in regards to
the women in my class, I will argue that the meaning of Chinese identity in Toronto should be seen as 'multiple, a site of
struggle, and subject to change' (Peirce 1995, 20). Considerable
diversity emerged in the contexts of our discussions and lessons,
and I believe this was result of each individual's response to the
particular familial and economic strains they were experiencing
or from which they were immune.[5]

Identifying the Variables: Family, Gender, Ethnicity, Class, and the State

Commitment to a notion of family is an extremely powerful source of motivation and identity. It is a commitment to not only a collective idea but also a particular set of responsibilities within hierarchical relations historically defined by men. This is not to say that Chinese women have been passive in light of global trends for empowerment, but rather that women's liberatory movements in China, as elsewhere, have been shaped by the unique, patriarchal priorities set by the various state governments in the region (e.g., Hong Kong, People's Republic of China, Taiwan). For instance, in the PRC following 1949, equality was largely defined as sharing in the labour necessary for socialist construction. The home front, however, has often been neglected as a serious locale for 'class struggle' resulting in the familiar scene of women labourers continuing to do the bulk of domestic work as well (see Davin 1976; Li 1987). Now, as China becomes increasingly stratified and capitalistic, benefits gained under the socialist constitution, such as guaranteed work and equal pay, may be given over to the whims and excesses of local managers.

In Hong Kong, we have what Rey Chow (1992) calls an 'anomaly' in the study of postcoloniality: 'a third space between the colonizer and the dominant native culture, a space that cannot simply be collapsed into the latter even as resistance to the former remains foremost' (Chow 1992, 158). For Hong Kong women, this ambiguity between 'the West' and 'the native land' must be negotiated in their work and family relationships. As in Canada, many of the younger generation compete in universities and in the job market, aspiring to the independence, large incomes, and forms of conspicuous consumption that characterize Hong Kong's feverish and layered prosperity. They are also delaying marriage and families, which is a bit of a shock to their elders. In contrast, according to the students in my class, a majority of the older generation define themselves, and their relative social status by their husbands' incomes. Most families in Hong Kong, if at all financially possible, prefer to have a mother at home with the children. Indeed, many of my students strongly believe that this is essential for the welfare of the children and their ability to complete their social and academic education successfully. Stated in such theoretical and impersonal terms, it is easy to lose sense of the devotion and satisfaction of the women in my class when they talk about taking care of their grandchildren, the accomplishments of their children, and the hopes for their families in Canada. Recently, this last idea has come under strain precisely because the foundation of patriarchal authority within the family has come under pressure from changes in the political economy of Canada.

Since 1988, Hong Kong has been the largest source of immigration to Canada (Thompson 1993). In 1992, 37,787 people from Hong Kong came to Canada, most of them settling in Toronto or Vancouver. That represents one-sixth of total immigration to the country. Most of these immigrants came as a result of their concerns over China's reacquisition of Hong Kong in 1997. Policy changes by our federal government have made immigration more possible for investors, in particular. Many other Hong Kong residents have successfully applied under our point system, which is weighted in favour of highly skilled and educated professionals. Other immigrants come under the family reunification program and must be sponsored by immediate family. In the investment and independent/point-system categories, we are generally selecting from the more affluent and elite sectors of Hong Kong society.

The combination of Canada's economic difficulties and the high expectations of newcomers – unduly reinforced by our government's point-system screening process – has resulted in frustration when Hong Kong immigrants find their options far more limited than previously expected. Systemic forms of discrimination in terms of assessment of professional training, work experience, and education persist in Ontario (see Burnaby 1992; Podoliak 1993). Those fortunate enough to find work are disappointed at their loss of income due to lower salaries and higher taxes compared to Hong Kong. Investors find the return on their investment and government and labour regulations a hindrance. The response for many has been to adopt the 'astronaut' lifestyle of commuting several times a year between Hong Kong and Toronto in order to maintain higher standards of living (Thompson 1993). The result has been large numbers of single-parent families and increases in divorce and family breakdowns (Thompson 1993). For families who have stayed together in Toronto, many women have entered the work force to help generate income for their families, sometimes becoming the sole means of support. Some are earning incomes comparable to or better than their husbands for the first time. Many women are taking ESL courses with the intention of seeking better employment opportunities. These responses to Canadian life have introduced new challenges to family relationships as they have been traditionally defined. In the context of identity formation, it is important to mention once again that national immigration policies do not select from a wide range of socioeconomic groups but tend to be narrowly focused. The manner in which gendered and classed values in one society articulate to dominant values in another will have an important influence on how immigrant identities are negotiated and whether specific families remain intact.

Lesson Plans

The following lesson, entitled 'Isolation,' comes from a students' text called *Decisions, Decisions* (Bowers and Godfrey 1985). I specifically selected it because it approximated the types of experiences intimated by my students during informal class discussions and touched on several of the settlement and familial pressures I have raised above. As well, it suited the high-intermediate level of this class. Each chapter in the book begins with a 'problem' followed by a number of controlled and relatively open activities that practice oral and written English:

> Yuen-Li is the wife of Chian-Li. They have been in the United States for two years. Chian-Li is very traditionally minded, believing that a wife should stay at home, make herself beautiful for him, and look after their two teenaged children, Steve and Sue. The family always speaks Cantonese at home, and Yuen-Li doesn't know any English. Chian-Li has attended English classes because sometimes

he needs English in his job. He is an importer. Yuen-Li feels very isolated. (Bowers and Godfrey 1985, 25)

After reading the passage, we concentrated on a group speaking activity focused on discussing and ranking appropriate solutions for Yuen-Li. What was particularly advantageous was the relative anonymity the exercise allowed for. While overtly providing advice for Yuen-Li, students could potentially introduce their own difficulties and beliefs with less fear of personal attribution and criticism from peers.[6] The structure of the activity thus enabled students to compare and reassess private experiences within a context of challenging alternatives that might otherwise have remained unspoken. The following solutions for Yuen-Li came from the text and were compared and evaluated by the class:

Solution No. 1. Try to explain to her husband that she, too, would like to take English classes.

Solution No. 2. Ask her children to try to convince Chian-Li that she should go to English classes.

Solution No. 3. Explain to Chian-Li that her lack of English will have a bad effect on the family.

Solution No. 4. Go to English classes during the day, and hope that Chian-Li will be pleased when he discovers that she has learned the language.

Solution No. 5. Find a hobby to pursue at home to keep herself occupied.

Solution No. 6. Get together with some friends who are in the same situation and employ a tutor to teach English to them in their homes.

Solution No. 7. Talk to some of the leaders of her ethnic community group and persuade them to start classes in English for housewives.

Solution No. 8. Other.

Solution No. 9. Other. (Bowers and Godfrey 1985, 26)

The discussions around the various solutions were quite animated and insightful. Most of the class preferred #3 for Yuen-Li as opposed to #1. All the students felt that to invoke family over individual needs would be the most powerful form of persuasion available. Three students liked #2 because they felt that Chian-Li was more likely to be persuaded by his children than by his wife. In regards to #4, two of the four men in the class stated that they would be angry if the option of 'secret lessons' were used in their households. In contrast, about half of the women felt that this was the best option, because it ensured that English would be learned, and it would increase Yuen-Li's opportunities in Canada. They often referred to the story's depiction of Chian-Li as 'traditionally minded' to state that it was unlikely that options #1 and #3 would change his mind.

One of the women in my class, an 'astronaut's widow,' got us all into fits of laughter with her repeated comments urging Yuen-Li to 'take power' from her husband. One of the men, currently unemployed and seeking work, replied that in Canada women have more power than men. His comment, noted for its quality of resentment, was elaborated on when I asked him to explain. He said that women can get jobs in Canada easier than men and thus had 'more power' in his estimation. He said that because the only jobs available at this time were for low pay, employers preferred to hire women, who were 'used to low wages' and would not leave at the first opportunity. I then tried to draw out opinions and experiences that would challenge his assumption and help indicate the constraints – the absence of power – that compel some women to stay in low-paying jobs. There appeared to be mixed sentiments concerning his evaluation. A couple of students stated that it was equally difficult for immigrant women to find work, especially for good wages. Another added that domestic duties, which husbands rarely shared in, often prevented immigrant women from seeking employment. Our class unanimously rejected option #5 and showed moderate interest for options #6 and #7.

When I asked for possible solutions other than the ones stated in the exercise, none were immediately volunteered. Since it was near the end of this class, I didn't try to pursue the possibility any further though, in retrospect, other suggested solutions would have contributed positively to our discussion. As well, more critical discussion of the existing solutions would have been helpful. For example, in regards to #7, how does one identify 'leaders' in the community? How is their authority established and exercised? Do they respond to the needs of all community members equally?

The next day I brought in a scripted dialogue that incorporated some of the ideas that were discussed the day before. I chose to elaborate on solution #4 because it had generated the most discussion and opposing viewpoints. From this discussion, I also sensed that this option personified the contradictions of changing identity in a way that the other solutions did not. In #4, Yuen-Li demonstrates individual courage and resistance (i.e., taking lessons without consent) on the one hand, yet caution and compliance to tradition (i.e., unwillingness to assert her independence or risk family unity) on the other, in the face of new social values and possibilities.

Prior to giving each student a copy, we reviewed many of the previous day's ideas and choices. I gave the dialogue to just one student, and we read it together. I then asked the class to determine which solution was being discussed. After a short discussion and repetition of the dialogue, I gave each student a copy.

Yuen: Sue, would you mind helping me cook dinner?
Chian: Yuen, you're speaking English. How did you learn those words?
Yuen: Oh, I've been studying at a community centre for several months. I really enjoy it, and the teacher is very good.
Chian: You should have told me first. You know that the customs here are different and you might cause some trouble for us.
Yuen: I'm sorry Chian. But you're so busy, and I didn't want to trouble you. Besides, the lessons are free, and many other Chinese housewives are in the class.
Chian: Well then, I think everything will be fine as long as you don't forget your duties for the family.

My initial objective for this scripted dialogue was to provide some guidance for lower-level students in my class who occasionally have trouble producing their own work. My intention was to place students together with partners who had expressed similar sentiments the day before and have them collaborate on a dialogue for presentation to the class. As mentioned earlier, I am interested in integrating pronunciation in as many activities as possible. Prior to placing students in pairs, I went over a few features of linking and palatalization in the scripted dialogue (e.g., 'Would you mind … How did you learn …'; the linking of $d + y$ producing the sound /dz/ like the 'j' in judge). I had a few students read the dialogue to the whole class followed by my corrections and comments. Two intonation patterns seemed unduly neglected, initially: Chian's surprise at hearing his wife speak English, and Yuen's response to her husband's surprise.

This became the unplanned focus of our lesson. To help explain what I felt was appropriate sentence-level intonation from a Hallidayan perspective, I needed to remind the students about the suggestions and responses from the previous day's lesson. To highlight the intonation resources available to the surprised husband, Chian, I asked the two male students who disliked the option of 'secret lessons' to reiterate their sentiments. This provided the social context necessary to elaborate on the semantic and functional potential of intonation. As mentioned in Halliday's (1985) discussion of tonality and tonicity, I organized the function of tonality through the following tone groups, or informational units, in my utterance: /Yuen/ You're speaking English/ How did you learn those words/. In the tone groups, I raised the entire pitch of my response relative to my normal voice, and provided the feature of tonicity, or tonic prominence, through strong emphasis and high-to-low falling tones on the stressed syllables of 'Yuen,' 'English,' and 'learn' to signal displeasure and surprise. Then I asked several other students to recall their reasons for choosing option #4 for Yuen. We referred to the issue of Chian's power and his 'traditional' thinking to debate the best strategy for Yuen at this juncture of the dialogue.

One single word became our focus: 'Oh'. Together we plotted strategies and possible intonation patterns to realize them. A fast rising tone by Yuen would probably indicate her uncertainty or questioning of Chian's response ('Why are you upset, Chian? Maybe I've done something wrong'). This response might indicate fear of Chian and/or a more covert form of resistance. A slow falling tone from a relatively high pitch would, in contrast, remove uncertainty. Such a contour, I suggested, could be used to indicate confidence in her decision, a way of dismissing Chian's concerns by implying 'Nothing unusual or inappropriate has happened here. All the other wives are studying, too.' These two patterns were practiced, and several of the students enjoyed placing particular emphasis on the social response that they wanted to convey. I realized that other contours were available for 'Oh' (rising-falling might indicate reiteration of an old dispute: 'You're bringing that issue up again.') but thought that it would be too difficult to include at this time.

This pattern of the lesson continued. We looked at each sentence, negotiating intonation patterns and particular words and phrases that would be most effective for Yuen. In Yuen's last response to Chian, we decided that particular emphasis (tonicity) must be placed on the following words (in italics): /you are *so busy*/ and I didn't want to *trouble* you/ /the lessons are *free*/ and *many other Chinese housewives*/ are in the class/. In this last example, some students opted for greater tonic prominence on the stressed syllable of 'many' while some chose 'Chinese' within the larger intonation focus of these four words. Both choices were interesting strategies to buttress Yuen's challenge to Chian's authority. The first one claims the force of numbers, while the second claims the force of ethnicity.

I had each student practice reading the scripted dialogues with a partner as I went around the room listening and offering suggestions regarding their use of intonation. For some students, the recognition of what to stress was not so easily transferable to how it might be done with larger elements of speech. In part, this may be a particular interlanguage problem common to speakers whose L1 uses tones phonemically to determine meanings at the level of a word (e.g., Mandarin, Cantonese, Vietnamese). Most of the class had little trouble altering their intonation to distinguish focal points, but did not achieve what would be termed native-English performance. I wasn't disappointed by this because my expectation was more inclined towards the recognition of potential rather than demonstration of mastery at this time. Most importantly, the students seemed to understand that intonation can play an important role in a strategic interaction between people and that its function in that interaction could be modified to reflect the social context in which it was transpiring.

Each pair of students then produced their own dialogues. I went around the room making suggestions and corrections. Each group presented their dialogues to the class with the added encouragement to remember and try to use the ideas about intonation that we had practiced. I have included two examples of their work with some errors retained that had eluded my earlier attention.

Yuen: Steve, can you do me a favour?

Steve: What can I do for you?

Yuen: Can you try to convince your father to let me go to English class?

Steve: Why do you want to learn English?

Yuen: I don't want stay at home all day long. I feel very isolated. On the other hand, if some accident happened there is no body at home, who can talk to the police or fireman.

Steve: You are right. I agree with you. I will talk my father, if you lack of English it will have a bad effect on our family. I will try to convince him.

Yuen: Thanks, Steve!

Steve: Don't mention it. It's my pleasure. That sounds great to me!

Yuen: I want to learn English in community centre. What do you think?

Chian: Do you have so much free time at home?

Yuen: No, if I don't know the English language, it's very inconvenient.

Chian: I think our family is more important than other things like English.

Yuen: Oh, no! I don't agree with you! I think if we don't know English, it will have a bad effect on our family.

Chian: This is a hard problem! Let me think late!

In reference to identity, it is interesting to recognize the weight placed upon familial obligations in these two dialogues. In the last dialogue, the extensive use of exclamation marks – unusual in any previous lesson – indicated a new awareness of the need to establish and integrate prosodic emphases along with lexical and grammatical strategies. Both dialogues were presented with great enjoyment near the end of our class.

In retrospect, I see a number of ways that this classroom activity could be expanded and improved. First, each group's composition/role play could be circulated throughout the class. Then the class could collectively negotiate 'appropriate' identity roles, tonicity and tonality as I had done with my own dialogue. In addition, the class could mark areas of tonicity on their copies as a listening activity prior to discussion. Again, to emphasize the *social* aspect in role play, I would focus on the types of questions that Halliday's notion of register might suggest: What are the 'rules' here? (How are they informed by culture, class, race or gender?) When, where, and why must they be obeyed? How can they be broken? What are the words, grammar forms, and intonation contours that enable this to happen?

Conclusions: Intonation, Gender, and the Negotiation of Power

> Men's language is the language of the powerful. It is meant to be direct, clear, succinct, as would be expected of those who need not fear giving offence, who need not worry about the risks of responsibility. It is the language of people who are in charge in the real world. Women's language developed as a way of surviving and even flourishing without control over economic, physical, or social reality. Then it is necessary to listen more than speak, agree more than confront, be delicate, be indirect, say dangerous things in such a way that their impact will be felt after the speaker is out of range of the hearer's retaliation. Robin Lakoff (1990, 205)

It would be inappropriate to tell students how to conduct their family lives in Canada. At the same time, I believe it would be irresponsible not to teach them how to 'say dangerous things' wherever and whenever they need to do so. As an ESL teacher, I am keenly interested in the full and yet unrealized potentials of language. Sometimes language is a thing of beauty, sometimes of clarity and precision, and sometimes it is a weapon. All local options of language should be made available to newcomers in our society – if not for personal use, then at least for scrutiny and recognition when their interests as newcomers are at stake. 'Saying dangerous things' is as much a condition of specific context and situation as it reflects generalized principles. This is where intonation – particularly within a Hallidayan perspective – seemed to play such an important part in our lesson. In the scripted dialogue, some of my students chose to use rising tones for 'Oh' because 'it is safer.' Others chose falling tones, making their 'deception' and challenge a little more explicit. For many of my students, these choices reflected their own conditions as much as the characters in the story.[7]

As suggested by Lakoff, the absence of power experienced by women is a reality that seeks out its own constrained resources. Sometimes it requires a radical and physical separation from past abuse and the repudiation of values that were previously central to one's identity. Other times, it may require finding ways to say dangerous and challenging things in modalities that *appear* delicate and indirect. The varied and subtle inflections of intonation seem consistent with the latter. Maybe this explains the noticeable enthusiasm for these lessons in my class. Will my students use their new understanding of ESL intonation to resist or challenge the roles ascribed to them in their family, particularly as family life in Canada undergoes transformation? Yes and no. On the one hand, spousal relationships are unlikely to be worked through in English. On the other, many children of immigrant families frequently speak English at home, rather than the mother tongue, and this often serves to isolate women such as Yuen-Li even further. So, in this regard, the kinds of situations presented in this lesson and in the student dialogues may well be relevant to broader communication patterns in immigrant families. Perhaps more importantly, our ESL classroom provided students with an opportunity to share their personal difficulties, evaluate them against the experiences of others, and begin to recognize them as socially constructed and potentially transformed through social action. We might see this process, and its active facilitation in our classes, as a primary means by which new solidarities and 'traditions' are developed within immigrant communities.

The dynamic aspects of intonation emerged as a focus of our lesson precisely because the social context that had been established – in many ways equally dynamic – served to demonstrate the meaning potential available through this aspect of the sound system. I believe this raises many challenging issues for the emerging concern of classroom research. Certainly, it suggests that ESL teachers pay close attention to the sociocultural backgrounds and needs of their particular students. A much more difficult challenge will be to uncover our own sociocultural assumptions embedded within our research approaches and the purposes for which we assign our findings. Will the scope of ESL teacher research be focused on accomplishing prefigured outcomes and standards more efficiently? Or, will inquiry include critical analyses of the knowledge forms we use in our classrooms and the social interests that these knowledge forms privilege? Similarly, will the purpose of action research be to increase our control over the idiosyncrasies of each classroom or, instead, to better anticipate the potential contribution of 'unexpected' events in developing lessons more relevant to students' experiences? It is worth repeating again that much of what happened in these lessons occurred not simply by chance but rather due to a willingness to risk linking previously disconnected ideas. The modest success of the results are a strong reminder that 'disconnected' ideas are more a product of a teacher's orientation and methods than any realities they might suggest.

Community Policing and the ESL Classroom

Introduction

This chapter came about as a response to a series of murders that occured within the immediate neighborhood of our school during 1991. Intensive media coverage at this time focused on the existence of Asian gangs competing over drug money, prostitution and gambling in Toronto's Chinatown. The sense of a 'rising tide of violence in Chinatown,' in the words of then Police Chief Mc-Cormack (O'Malley 1991), was also compounded by reports in the media of difficulties the police had in gathering information and finding witnesses to crimes. Were they dealing with a 'language barrier' or an alternative set of evaluations of the situation that might be termed 'cultural miscommunication'? The issues and contexts were complex, and the effect on our local community was evidenced by the growing reluctance of some of my students to venture from their homes in the evening. Clearly, increased crime in a community can produce isolation, which in turn allows crime to flourish. Along with such truisms, it's important to remember that the choice to remain isolated is often a preferred response when public authority is perceived, fairly or otherwise, to be either uninterested or unable to solve the problem.

These lessons provided an opportunity for each student to hear how other students were coping with the situation, what kinds of personal and sociocultural experiences influenced their actions, and what kinds of solutions they would collectively find most effective. In the course of our lessons, I hoped we would explore a number of interdependent issues: 1) Comparative sociocultural experiences and expectations of crime and policing; 2) Comparative experiences of the responsibilities of citizens in supporting law enforcement; 3) The security of the family versus security of the community; 4) 'Real' and perceived experiences of overt/covert, individual/systemic racial prejudice experienced by a minority group in contact with authority (i.e., police, government bureaucracies).

Many unique insights can be gained from a 'comparative' vantage point as outlined above. For example, when we talk about crime *in* society, we implicitly demonstrate that 'breaking' the law conforms to larger 'laws' or shared expectations amongst criminals, citizens, and police officers within a specific community defined by race, ethnicity, class, and gender. Criminals often prey upon their own social group because they are able to induce fear and silence in ways that are largely inscrutable to 'outsiders.' Students in my class have, on occasion, described acts of extortion in local restaurants, where no words were exchanged and no papers furtively passed beneath the table. Clearly, a restricted code of messages was involved, requiring translation as if it were a foreign language. Of course, there is a similar element of cultural expectation and predictability that enables police to evaluate motives, prevent crimes, and apprehend criminals. At the same time, if policing assumptions and strategies are found to be ineffectual in a culturally diverse setting, then there is also the potential for frustrated officers 'seeing' potential criminals in every encounter with a specific minority group or questioning that same group's commitment to crime prevention.

In a comparative perspective, one also recognizes that laws and their enforcement, in some societies, are primarily and explicitly concerned with protecting the interests of privileged elites – and often through excessive coercion and violence. For some new Canadians, the notion of providing information, appearing as a witness, or assisting authority in any way lacks the altruistic motivations familiar to many Canadians, particularly if the police are perceived to be insensitive or hostile to specific minority groups.

These are the types of interrelated social considerations that make policing in a multicultural community such as Toronto particularly difficult. The important point for ESL practice, I believe, is not to trivialize or belittle such experiences and responses, but rather to provide a classroom forum where students and teachers collectively evaluate the potential consequences of individual (in)action for the individual, the family, and the community.

Lesson Plans

The class that participated in the following lessons was of a high-intermediate level at our community center. Of the sixteen students in the class, six were from Hong Kong, three from mainland China, two from Vietnam, two from Ethiopia, one from Sri Lanka, one from Japan, and one from Belize. Having this diversity provided students with many different frames of reference with which either to reevaluate or to strengthen their own actions and beliefs. At the same time, many of the 'lively' classroom discussions underlined the differences of opinions and motivations that exist within ethnic groups assumed to be homogeneous. Experiences of class and gender were often more discernible than ethnicity in building small coalitions of support in classroom debates.

LESSON 1: Speaking activity (two hours)
Students were first put into small groups to discuss the following questions which were written on the blackboard:

1) What are the causes of the increase in crime in Chinatown? (Make a list.)
2) Has this caused any changes in your lifestyle?
3) What are some solutions for this problem? (Make a list.)

Teacher's Note: Various grammatical, functional, and notional items can be incorporated here and briefly discussed prior to the group discussion. (perhaps 15 to 30 minutes). 'Making suggestions,' 'interrupting politely,' and 'expressing opinions' are possible functions to incorporate with grammatical structures and markers. For lower-level students, question #2 could incorporate 'personal emotions' using verbs such as 'be' and 'feel,' which connect predicate adjectives with their subjects.

The advantage of pre-activity structural description versus post-speaking emphasis is that it will encourage some students to participate who are otherwise reluctant to risk public examination of their errors. It also provides the teacher with an opportunity to connect past structural and functional lessons to new situations. This provides an important counterbalance to the frequent separation of 'form' from 'purpose,' which often inhibits students from transferring new skills beyond the limited contexts in which they have been introduced. Both pre-speaking and post-speaking structural activities are useful. The latter should depend on the types of problems that the teacher observes during group discussion. An excellent reference for integrating language items with tasks is Nunan's Syllabus Design *(1988).*

After about thirty minutes, I compiled a list of 'causes' (question #1) as produced by the small groups and wrote them on the board for the entire class to discuss. I made several corrections in grammar and asked students to clarify chosen vocabulary items (e.g., anonymous, capital punishment, materialism) in the following:

1) Too many immigrants/refugees coming to Canada (not well educated).
2) The economy in Canada is very bad. People are losing their jobs.
3) In Chinatown, people can become anonymous.
4) It's easy to buy a gun in Canada/U.S.A. (A gun culture/violence culture).
5) No capital punishment in Canada.
6) Not enough police.
7) People are afraid to stand up or be a witness (afraid of revenge).
8) Typical big city problems: crowded, drugs.
9) People desire more and more. They are materialistic.

Here is a list of 'solutions' produced by the class:

1) More police.
2) Stricter laws and punishment.
3) Change lifestyle: become a witness/brave citizen.
4) Stricter immigration; stricter border control.
5) More government support for poor people: more jobs.
6) More education for teenagers: proper behaviour, citizenship, responsibility.
7) No violent movies on television.

After I compiled the above lists, I asked students to talk about their choices and things that they remembered from the group discussions. The large group activity enabled students to produce new ideas through interaction and reflect upon their own choices when alternative perspectives were discussed. For example, after examining the above lists, students were able to see that crime has both 'symptoms' and 'sources.' To incarcerate people longer and more often does not necessarily reduce crime if there are no jobs in a community. Some students who had previously expressed singular solutions were now less committed to them. The unique perspectives of newcomers allowed many of them to focus on related social and cultural causes of crime that native-born Canadians rarely consider pertinent. The excessive materialism of our society, the violence on television, and the inadequate education of our youth were passionate themes in the discussion. For the last fifteen minutes of our class, I wrote one question on the board to complement our discussion: 1) Who is responsible for each problem and solution: the individual, the family, or leaders in the community?

One discussion in particular underlined the complexity of the related issues and the intolerance associated with them. This discussion referred to 'cause' #1, which was listed on the board. While it might seem unusual for new Canadians to suggest that there are 'too many immigrants/refugees' coming here, in reality the issue was a struggle over the meanings associated with both terms. Which students would be associated with the 'criminal element?' Who could claim higher status in the self-perceived hierarchy of newcomers to Canada?

Lurid headlines such as 'Restaurant mayhem' (*Globe and Mail*) or 'Shooting it out in Chinatown' (*Toronto Star*) had engendered considerable resentment amongst local residents. Similarly, when a police detective is publicly quoted as saying that he 'avoids Chinatown altogether' because innocent bystanders are going to be hurt (Mallet 1993, 38), local merchants are rightly concerned that their customers will no longer support their businesses. Public pressure soon mobilizes for quick solutions and easily identifiable culprits. Such publicity only exacerbates the internal Asian 'class' system in which some Chinese condescend towards Vietnamese, many of whom are refugees, and see them as primarily responsible for crime in the community. Mallet's article encourages such an attitude with her unusual and dubious characterization of the Vietnamese as 'a subculture of the Chinese (many Vietnamese are ethnic Chinese)' (Mallet 1993, 33). No doubt, the 'objective' criteria with which Mallet constitutes an 'authentic' culture would be found problematic. As well, what Mallet avoids examining in this comment are the complex reasons *why* ethnic Chinese, or any bounded social group, for that matter, actively maintain this boundary over generations, resisting intermarriage, local schools, and the majority language.

The ESL classroom, invariably, becomes the site where conflicting histories and identities encounter each other. Originally, some students wanted to exclude 'immigrants' from the 'cause' list while others, in particular two refugees in my class, asked for its inclusion. One student from Hong Kong suggested that the criminals were all refugees from either Vietnam or mainland China. In her estimation, by being a refugee one has shown a propensity towards violating authority of one kind or another. A student from China responded that the 'bosses are from Hong Kong.' He then raised his hands in the pose of a gunslinger and exclaimed, 'Hong Kong, boom boom' to the uproarious laughter of the class. The Hong Kong student indignantly countered that because there are records of crime in Hong Kong, no Hong Kong criminals could possibly get into Canada as immigrants. Another student replied that criminals with money don't have records because they can buy powerful friends. This student believed that it was the responsibility of the government to find out *how* applicants for Canada's investment immigration program acquired their wealth.

It was indeed a lively discussion and an extremely important debate, for it challenged the legitimacy of many common-sense assumptions held by some students, which were resented by others. As well, it emphasized the wide range of issues that come to influence crime and crime prevention. Another memorable comment, which had widespread support, referred to our prison system: 'too expensive and too comfortable.' Also, one student suggested that the government introduce 'secret witnessing,' anonymous phone-in reports of suspected criminal activity. In response, one student disagreed saying it was 'just like the Cultural Revolution.' The issue of responsibility, with specific reference to 'solution' #3 (becoming a 'witness' or a 'brave' citizen), generated many diverse opinions that would be developed later.

LESSON 2: Reading exercise (approximately three hours)
Pre-reading speaking activity. Group work on the following questions:

1) Have you ever spoken to a police officer? Why? How did you feel?
2) In your native country, did the police do a good job of law enforcement?
3) As a child, what lessons did you learn about law enforcement and police work?
4) Do citizens have a responsibility to help the police in their work?

Teacher's Note: Pre-reading activities are important for facilitating a variety of literacy strategies. They encourage the ways in which readers will interact with a text and the types of meanings and uses that are produced as a result of this interaction. With that in mind, it is useful for teachers to consider the perspectives that they hope to strengthen with their selection of reading material before they develop relevant pre-reading activities.

*To illustrate, I will refer to a model of 'literacy phases' by Ada
(adapted by Cummins 1989a, 73–5). These are: 1) a descriptive phase;
2) personal interpretive phase; 3) critical analysis phase; 4) creative
action phase. For example, question #3 above encourages a 'descriptive'
engagement with text – what happened, where, and when? Question
#1 would encourage the types of experiential meanings referenced by
a 'personal interpretive' phase. Question #2 encourages 'critical analysis' of student experiences by using the available resources of the
ESL classroom – the students. Individual judgement on policing can
be evaluated with greater clarity after comparison with a diversity of
student experiences. Again, the significant point for literacy training is
the process of comparing various experiences/texts in order to ascertain
the validity of a particular perspective and the social interests which
are promoted by this representation. Finally, question #4 links language
activity to participation in community life. Ideas and comparative perspectives introduced in the class create potential for motivating 'creative
action' amongst students. For example, classroom discussion might
simply prompt some students to seek advice from the local police about
protecting their homes and businesses from vandalism.*

The pre-reading discussion generated many ideas that reflected
on my own assumptions about policing. In contrast to many of
my students, I have never felt fear around police officers. As a
son of a lawyer, I was often introduced to police officers. As well,
police officers periodically came to our schools as part of their
community-relations activities (four of my students said that they
had never spoken to a police officer in any environment). In the
past, I have personally made a complaint against an officer and
would not hesitate to ask an officer for his or her badge number if I
felt that something improper had occurred. This sense of treating
a police officer as a social equal has been formed by my personal
experiences and privileges of class, ethnicity, race, and gender. As
well, my confidence around an officer is not something hidden
but embodied in language and physical presence that, in turn,
promotes the social equality that I presume.

Many ESL students fear any contact with the police, if not the
entire criminal-justice system. As indicated during our discussion,

some students believe that an individual police officer, lawyer, or government official has the power to deport people arbitrarily to their place of origin regardless of their status as refugee, landed immigrant, or citizen. Many students raised concerns that they would be treated unfairly by the police and the courts if they ever dared to question the conduct of an officer. Many of these ideas, of course, are the legacy of abusive authority in students' native countries. Yet some student fears have been reinforced or even formed here in Canada. Such concerns were substantiated in a provincial study on systemic racism in Ontario's criminal-justice system. In reference to the study, Judge David Cole said, 'A perception remains that [minorities] *are* sentenced more harshly by judges and singled out because of their background' (emphasis in original, Tyler 1993, A2). Of course, such a perception is likely to discourage minority citizens from participating in the security of their neighbourhoods.

Several other comments about policing generated interesting class discussions. In several countries, police officers are paid so poorly that it is routine for local merchants to provide added 'support' to ensure the safety that we take for granted in Toronto. According to some students, private security is the preferred option in some communities, creating increased circulation of weapons and the danger of summary justice and retribution. Everyone agreed that good pay and good education are important prerequisites for an effective police force.

Reading Assignment

The following story about Wendy (a pseudonym) was adapted from a real incident that happened to a colleague of mine. I gave each student a copy of the story to read silently and underline any words, phrases or ideas that they were unsure of.

> Wendy Chow is a landed immigrant from Hong Kong. She has been living in Toronto for fifteen years. Although her English is excellent, she still has a strong accent. Sometimes, she is uncomfortable when she is talking to strangers.

One day, she got into a car accident on her way home from work. Another woman driver pulled out of a gas station and hit the side of Wendy's car. Wendy's car was badly damaged. At first, the other driver wanted to forget the whole thing. She claimed that Wendy's car was too old and that the police were not needed to solve the problem.

Wendy felt that this woman was very rude. She insisted that they call a police officer to the scene. When the policemen came, the other driver ran over and talked to the officer for ten minutes. After that, Wendy wanted to tell her side of the story, but the policemen told her that it wasn't necessary. 'Just give me your licence.' The policemen told Wendy not to worry because the accident was not her fault. Later, at the insurance company, Wendy's agent expressed surprise that the policeman had not laid criminal charges or even issued a ticket against the other driver. This comment upset Wendy. Maybe the agent believed that Wendy had not told the truth. Wendy now feels that she was a victim of discrimination. She hasn't been able to sleep and has had stomach problems since the incident. Her friends have asked her to complain to the Human Rights Commission or to the police, but she refuses because she is scared of seeing either the policeman or the other driver.

I had several students each read a paragraph of the story. We discussed vocabulary, grammar structures, and idiomatic items. I asked several 'descriptive phase' questions related to the story (e.g., Why does Wendy feel she was a victim of discrimination?) as well as 'critical analysis'/'personal interpretive' types (e.g., Was this a language problem? Cultural miscommunication? Discrimination? Why?). I told the class that this was a true story and asked them to think about possible solutions for Wendy's predicament. I then wrote the following post-reading exercise on the board for small-group work:
1) Make a list of the choices Wendy has for solving her problem.
2) What are the possible consequences for each choice?

Teacher's Note: Prior to discussion, I reviewed several structures that can be used to express 'possibility' and 'probability' for question #2.

'Giving Advice' is a functional focus that could be easily incorporated for #1. Again, with a mixed-level class I will introduce or reintroduce structures that vary in graded difficulty. For example, modals are presented along with adverbs, conditionals, and structures such as adjective complements or 'that' clauses/complements. I always point out to the class that there are many different structures that can be used for the same purpose. For lower-level students, I try to encourage them to concentrate only on a few structures, which can be successfully used in the immediate task. For my own grammar reference, I often use Celce-Murcia and Larsen-Freemen (1983).

The following list was produced by the class. I wrote it on the board and asked the groups to discuss their choices and the possible outcomes that they considered.

1) Go to the Human Rights Commission.
2) She should hire a lawyer.
3) Go to the newspapers and complain about the policeman.
4) Complain to the police department.
5) She should have insisted on talking to the policeman until the situation was solved.
6) Write a letter to the government.
7) Do nothing (Forget it).

In terms of 'problem posing,' discussion on the class list provided the best opportunity to direct attention to the interconnection of individual rights with community responsibilities. One student, a young man from Sri Lanka, spoke about the consequences of #7: 'Don't let people take away your rights. They are in the constitution.' In contrast, supporters of option #7 claimed that 'all the other choices are useless' or 'a waste of time and money.' Another student, an elderly woman from Hong Kong, countered, 'If you do nothing, things will be worse next time for immigrants.' Many students agreed. This last comment and consensus framed the issue in a way that emphasized that one's inaction has active and adverse consequences for others in a community. Several subsequent statements indicated that this linked perspective was influential. A student who had earlier said that she would never assist the police commented, 'If I was a witness, I would do something.' When I pointed out the change she replied, 'I'm scared of revenge. For a car accident I'm a witness; for a robbery, I'm not.'

Pointing out the apparent contradictions of my student's statement, here, was not intended to invalidate either her response or belittle her opinions. Instead, I wanted to emphasize that the difficulties and opposing sentiments she experienced are ones to which we all are potentially subject. Hopefully, this difficult process of examining our conflicting interests and responsibilities in the classroom might provide a more realistic framework with which to scrutinize the effectiveness of future policies on community policing. Ignoring such contradictions could have the opposite effect. Option #7 was clearly the most contentious and divided issue in the class. The absence of unanimity in this case was not a disappointment, because the passionate discussion was a wonderful opportunity for students to clarify or reevaluate ideas and language skills.

Opposition to #2 was concentrated on the high cost of a lawyer regardless of the outcome of the complaint. Alternatively, one of my Ethiopian students liked #3 because it 'doesn't cost any money, and you won't get into trouble.' 'Trouble' was a recurring theme, which discouraged many students from options #4 and #5. Both options provided an opportunity to discuss and compare perceptions of the checks and balances on law enforcement in Toronto. Against option #4, one student said, 'Police departments protect the police.' Another student disagreed: 'The police *will* discipline the officer.'

For the final ten minutes of the class I asked everyone to select the best and worst choice for Wendy. Here are the results of a poll conducted by show of hands:

1) Go to the Human Rights Commission. Best 4 / Worst 0
2) She should hire a lawyer. B 0 / W 8
3) Go to the newspapers and complain about the policeman. B 2 / W 0
4) Complain to the police department. B 1 / W 0

5) She should have insisted on talking to the policeman until the situation was solved. B 3 / W 0
6) Write a letter to the government. B 2 / W 0
7) Do nothing (Forget it). B 4 / W 5

Teacher's Note: The last activity could be done in group work incorporating a review of functional materials on 'negotiation,' 'persuasion,' and polite and impolite(!) forms of 'disagreement.' While the latter function is something to be discouraged in the classroom, the ability to recognize 'aggressive' or 'exclusionary' forms of language is often a necessary social skill.

From our discussion and the results of the poll, it is noteworthy to point out the low esteem my students accorded the legal profession. During our discussion, I sometimes bristled at comments made about lawyers and, on occasion, defended the good intentions and 'modest' incomes that some Canadian lawyers have. Not surprisingly, some students have transferred this negative sentiment onto politicians, a majority of whom receive their training and world view from the legal profession.

LESSON 3: Role play (approximately two hours)
I made the following role play dialogue after our discussions on Lesson #2. Prior to giving each student a copy, I had one student join me to present the dialogue to the other students. After we did it twice, I asked the students which 'choices' they recognized from the previous day's lesson. I then gave each student a copy of the dialogue.

> Friend: Wendy, you look terrible. What's the problem?
> Wendy: Oh, I'm still upset about that car accident. I can't believe all the trouble I got into. I wish I had never driven a car in my whole life.
> F: Why do you say that? Other people get into accidents. You shouldn't just stay home and feel sorry for yourself.
> W: Well, what can I do? The insurance agent doubts my story and the policeman didn't press charges against the other motorist.

F: Yes, that was a mistake. You should have insisted that the policeman listen to your story.

W: Sure! That's easy for you to say! I was scared.

F: But look at you now. You're having trouble sleeping at night and you've been grumpy at work.

W: It's just awful! I feel that I've been discriminated against and I can't do anything about it.

F: No, that's not true. If I were you, I would go to the Human Rights Commission and complain.

W: Are you kidding? What if the policeman finds out? He'll come around and cause lots of trouble.

F: No, you have nothing to worry about.

W: Wrong. I have a family to worry about. I'm just going to forget the whole thing.

After answering questions on vocabulary, grammar, and general content, I asked several pairs of students to read the dialogue out loud to the class. I focused my comments and corrections on pronunciation skills at a sentence and phrase level with emphasis on intonation, stress patterns, linking, and contractions. I then assigned each student to a partner and had them read the dialogue out loud, paying careful attention to the pronunciation patterns that I discussed. As I went from pair to pair, I also had an opportunity to make a few corrections on individual problems with specific consonant and vowel sounds. After about ten minutes, I wrote the following assignment on the blackboard: 'With your partner, write a dialogue for Wendy and a friend. Use one or two of the "suggestions" from yesterday's class.'

I told the students that they would present their dialogues at the end of the class. I noted some of the differences between spoken and written language. I said that 'dialogue' is a word which refers to an exchange of ideas between people, as opposed to a monologue. As well, I mentioned that contractions are far more common in spoken speech and generally absent from written texts. I also asked the class to go over their dialogues orally to check for pronunciation problems prior to presentation. For the next half hour I went around the class, first helping students with content and structure and then later with pronunciation. Finally, each group presented their dialogue. I gave the class the 'option' of reading from their scripts, which all of them chose to do. After each dialogue, we asked the presenters questions pertaining to the content, and I made final comments about pronunciation.

Teacher's Note: The artificiality of 'pre-constructing' a dialogue is considerable. The absence of spontaneity eliminates the need to incorporate listening strategies. The negotiation and persuasion that develop between dyad partners during dialogue scripting compensate in some ways, however. The reason I find this activity valuable is that it allows me to monitor individual structural and pronunciation needs more closely, which can be quite diverse in a continuous intake or multi-streamed program (for a good pronunciation reference, see Avery and Ehrlich 1992). If time permits, I sometimes have students present dialogues a second time – but without the script present. In this way, students have an inventory to fall back on as well as the opportunity to expand spontaneously on their ideas. Of course, listening skills then become essential for appropriate responses.

The following examples were presented to the class. I have included errors from these 'final' copies, which were given to me after presentation for additional correcting. As a result of my earlier contributions in the compositional stages of the dialogues, these errors are an incomplete representation of the students' abilities but they do give an indication of the general level of the students and the types of structural activities that can be developed for later lessons.

Dialogue 1
Friend: Wendy, how about your car accident?
Wendy: I'm still nervous about that accident. I'd never experienced such a worst situation. I'm afraid that I'll never drive again.
F: Don't be still upset about that car accident, Wendy!
W: Well! What can I do? No one believes my story because I didn't have a chance to talk with the police at the scene. All the evidences are given by the other driver.

F: I advise you'd better go to the Human Rights commission and complain.

W: Oh no! I did think about it. However, I'm afraid of being given trouble by the police.

F: Can you forget the whole story, Wendy?

W: Of course! The best idea is to forget it.

Dialogue 2

Friend: I heard you got into a car accident. Was it serious?

Wendy: Yes, my car was seriously damaged, but I haven't gotten any compensation from the insurance agency, and they also said I was not telling the truth.

F: How come?

W: That policeman told me that it was not my fault, but the other driver didn't get a traffic ticket. The policeman didn't do anything to her.

F: Obviously, you were discriminated by the policeman. You could go to the Human Rights Commissioner to complain.

W: I was scared to face this problem. I want to forget it.

F: No, if you do that, you will just show your weakness and you will lose confidence in your life. You should stand up against the discrimination. That's your right. Don't give up.

W: Thank you for your suggestion. I am going to the Human Rights Commissioner immediately.

Dialogue 3

Friend: Wendy, you look unhappy. What's wrong?

Wendy: I'm still thinking about the car accident. I wish I had never driven the car in my life.

F: Why? How can you stay home and feel sorry for yourself?

W: But what can I do? My car was damaged that's true, but the agent didn't trust me and the policeman didn't charge that driver.

F: Yes, that's true. But if I were you, I would hire a lawyer.

W: Sure! That's easy for you to say, if I have enough money. But I can't because I can just make ends meet and I have no extra money to hire a lawyer to solve the problem.

F: But look at you now. You're having trouble sleeping at night.

W: I feel that I got no respect from the policeman and he had discriminated against me.

F: No, that's not true. Why don't you complain to the police department?

W: Are you kidding? You know, I can't explain myself in English fluently, how can I complain?

F: No. You are wrong, you can ask a friend who can speak English fluently to help you.

W: Can you help me?

F: I'm sorry, my English is not good enough to help you. Why don't you ask [another student] to help you?

W: O.K. that's a good idea. I will try it. Thanks a lot.

The class dialogues provided important insights into the interdependent issues of responsibility and the effects of perceived discrimination by authority. Many students felt that Wendy's predicament had simply been a case of 'cultural misunderstanding' between the police officer and Wendy: Wendy had overreacted to events that could have easily been resolved through discussion with the police officer or the police department's community-relations staff. Some said that the problem of discrimination may be with the insurance agent. Either way, the inaction resulting from Wendy's fear – shared by many classmates – had the same effect as if she had been a victim of overt discrimination. By not seeking answers or redress, Wendy had made her perceptions a reality which, in the future, would discourage her participation in the collective security of her community. In this way, the repercussions of Wendy's problem are shared by the entire community.

Teaching and Learning with 'Strings Attached'

Many opportunities for related research came about from these classroom activities. In retrospect, perhaps the most surprising issue in these lessons was the degree of restraint and inaction induced by the potential for revenge. Many Chinese students, especially my colleague 'Wendy,' conducted themselves in a way which, on one hand, seemed excessively self-protective and, on the other, suggested that there were unique sociocultural experiences involved that I should examine before passing judgement. Of note, Yang defines the Chinese cultural practice of *pao* as the obligation 'to respond, to repay, to retaliate and to retribute' (Yang 1957, 291). According to Yang, Chinese culture has traditionally placed a high value on balancing and reciprocating one's emotional and material relationships. Furthermore, he notes that the obligation of response can be jointly shared by a family or a neighbourhood and that the expectation of balance can be for generations. If such historical practices were in any way influential upon contemporary events, it would help explain the added responsibilities that individuals would weigh before seeking legal recourse against others, particularly individuals in positions of authority.

The fear of retribution, in this perspective, indicates a legitimate concern that sheds light on how criminal behaviour can be grafted upon cultural practices. Threats upon one's family, or the potential thereof, become even more frightening when one considers King's (1991) discussion of the relative predominance of family relationships in the formation of Chinese social identity. Such concerns would place added burden upon law enforcement in a multicultural society: When is police protection from a potential act of retribution legitimate? When does such surveillance constitute a violation of an individual's rights? These are difficult and challenging questions, which also give an indication of the motivations that discourage some citizens from participating in the security of their community.

The discussions and dialogues generated other important considerations for community development. Many of the strategies I used in class were designed to parallel the way public decisions are formulated, mobilized, or resisted through language in the greater society. For example, we looked at some of the language resources used to develop arguments, support one's own position, and critically evaluate 'competing' texts (see Hunter and Cooke 1988). And not unlike legal and political processes in our society, we spent some time collectively appraising individual actions and beliefs, particularly their potential consequences for the community. It is worth considering, in this perspective, the implicit social values that are referenced by the classroom activities I've incorporated. Group discussions, hierarchical ranking of 'choices,' the language of 'negotiation' and 'compromise' index particular cultural values and elite interests that, in the context of law enforcement, promote the notion of social justice as an absolute, universal truth attained through reasoned debate amongst an impartial citizenry and its legal specialists. Personal biases and social power relations, in this equation, dissipate under the illuminating gaze of dispassionate, rational discourse.

With this is mind, it could be suggested that an uncritical application of the 'debate' format in the ESL classroom promotes an expectation – on the part of refugees, immigrants, *and* ESL instructors – that all legitimate interests will be equally evaluated and protected by the 'objective' assessment of their respective, individual merits. As noted above in the study on Ontario's legal justice system, that is not always the case. Full equality before the law remains a noble goal rather than a reality. More importantly, the necessary financial and political resources required to formulate, administer, or circumvent legal policy are essential prerequisites for legal 'equality.' Indeed, contemporary Canadian politics is replete with various media-focused interest groups organized to put pressure on government to develop laws exclusive to their constituencies. By their actions, such groups recognize that the law is not an abstract entity outside of society but, instead, a creation of society reflecting competing and changing social interests.

Of course, it would be quite unusual to discourage the use of classroom procedures that I consistently apply in my own program. Rather, my intention in this discussion is to re-emphasize the notion of 'dialogue' (see Chapter 1) to help us critically reflect upon what we do and what we expect in our classrooms. Methods and materials that teachers effortlessly impose upon their students always have the *potential* of fostering social values and aspirations from which ESL learners are realistically excluded. The word 'potential' requires emphasis here because it is both presumptuous and arrogant to ignore the fact that many learners are more aware than their teachers of the 'unintended' modes of conformity inherent in the carousel of innovations brought before them. Not surprisingly, some of these students make their awareness publicly known during the course of a lesson.

In my own experience, repeated during the lessons on 'Wendy's' dilemma, I reminded myself to resist the initial temptation towards dismissing unwanted and unexpected student responses. Students who view 'negotiation' and 'debate' as 'useless,' in this perspective, may not be purposely disrupting a teacher's well-thought out lesson plans. In fact, they may be offering insights and realistic appraisals of the various ways that specific language practices promote or sustain special interests. Instead of avoiding the debate format in an ESL classroom, it becomes more appropriate to incorporate student skepticism and resistance as an essential component of the lesson: Why do some students consider public discussion ineffectual? Are there examples in our political and legal institutions that substantiate our students' concerns? What can teachers and students learn from such examples? In this way, the contradictory nature of 'debate' and 'negotiation' becomes foregrounded in the classroom and linked to the greater society. The lesson can then explore two sides of the same coin: that public debate in our political and legal institutions has the potential for creative and equitable resolutions of serious social problems; and that it can also serve as a means to defer or avoid making difficult policy decisions that have a direct bearing on the lives of new Canadians.

As noted by Cooke, English is indeed a 'language with strings attached.' Teachers have an important responsibility to reflect critically and explicitly upon the culture of power in which we reside:

> The challenge for language teachers is that if it is difficult to avoid exporting our culture and ideology, it becomes essential for us to interpret them to our learners in as critical a fashion as possible. Moreover, if it is valid to be aware of cultural intrusion in foreign settings, it is just as true back home in ESL and ESD. Immigrants to English Canada, whether from Quebec or overseas, are entering the

world of Anglophone Canada and its dominant ideology. They may
or may not wish to be part of it, but they are certainly enveloped in
it. Whether they agree with it or not, they should know its nature.
(Cooke 1988, 31)

Cooke goes on to make an observation that I feel is essential for
responsible ESL teaching: 'Interestingly, a critical approach to the
values within our own language and culture should also make us
aware of *other* cultures' (emphasis his, 31). In the spirit of this comment, and in the framework of this chapter, I wish to draw upon
my observations, experiences, and intuitions regarding some of
the challenges for effective community policing in a multicultural
society.

Many conflicting sentiments characterized our classroom discussions on policing and law enforcement. Students who believed
that police officers were insensitive to their cultural community
and unable to understand or control 'ethnic' crime also felt that
more officers and stricter laws offered an effective solution. When
queried, the extent to which some hoped law enforcement would
expand included the types of measures that would be considered
dracononian by conventional Canadian standards and, ironically,
characterize the types of governments from which many immigrants and refugees have escaped. Certainly, many established
Canadians have similar sentiments about authority. What is interesting to point out, however, is that there is limited consensus
about which types of 'offences' deserve harsher punishment. In
fact, in a comparative cultural perspective it becomes apparent
that there are quite diverse understandings of the boundaries between illegal, unethical, and ethical social conduct.

The boundary here becomes extremely important when one
reflects upon the dominant socialization processes in Canadian
life. If the appearance from outside of Canada is one of minimal police presence and noticeably lax laws, then one might also
wonder how our society avoids slipping into civil chaos. The
answer would seem that a large majority of Canadians either
actively participate in the security of their communities or recognize such participation as a responsibility of citizenship. This

is not to suggest that Canadians are uniquely altruistic or compassionate, but that they have internalized an ideology or discourse regarding law enforcement and their responsibilities towards its maintenance. Moreover, these internalized values can be seen to reflect unequal relations of social power. Simply subject yourself to a week of television sitcoms and local newspapers and then make note of how many drug dealers are apprehended and incarcerated in comparison to board chairs whose corporations have irreparably polluted the environment or whose private interests are vigorously pursued regardless of the negative consequences to the general society. Examples abound of the various explicit and implicit messages that maintain the tenuous border between criminal versus noncriminal behaviour. I use the word tenuous here because it is clear that the ideology of shared security is primarily sustained through a general consensus in which members of the community see themselves equally as beneficiaries. When this consensus breaks down, as eloquently detailed by Galbraith (1992), then security becomes increasingly fragmented, individualized, and ultimately ineffective. No amount of police surveillance or incarceration, in Galbraith's view, can compensate for the misguided policies, economic marginalization, and resulting violence that increasingly characterize many North American urban centres.

The growing disaffection and cynicism with our political and legal institutions is marked specifically by their departure from the social ideal or central organizing myths of the society. That is, we expect – more importantly, we are socialized to expect – the universal application of law in our society. Not unlike other societies, our authorities periodically provide sacrificial lambs, such as the imprisoned broker, Ivan Boesky, in a ritualistic reinforcement of the notion that it is morally corrupt individuals who threaten social 'equality' – never the system. In contrast, many students come from societies where bureaucracies and institutions are not expected to provide ethical consistency with each set of circumstances (see Yang 1957), particularly when narrow elite interests are exclusively represented and enforced. Instead, individuals and families are compelled to rely upon informal networks and alliances with reciprocal obligations that allow them to obtain favourable conditions in their lives (see Boissevain 1985; King 1991). Moreover, benefits derived exclusively from one's strong social network are not necessarily perceived as transgressions of the general community's well-being. Otherwise, the government would arbitrarily use the necessary and readily available power to change the situation. In fact, special privileges derived from one's network affiliations may be seen as successful examples for other individuals or social networks to emulate.

In multicultural settings such as Toronto, Vancouver, or Montreal, such observations provide an interesting context for the complexities of nurturing a sense of shared responsibility for security. Significantly, we should not assume that cultural groups transpose their experiences directly onto the Canadian scene. It was the anthropologist Gregory Bateson (1972) who emphasized that in order to understand the forms of interaction produced *between* different sociocultural groups, it is necessary to understand how such groups differentiate or stratify themselves *within*. Internal social relationships – the ways in which societies 'separate' the men from the boys, the men from the women, the powerful from the weak, the rich from the poor, can be accentuated or modified as a result of interaction with other cultural groups.

In a phenomenon typical of many immigrant societies, new Canadians seek acceptance and approval within the terms of the dominant society: sending their children to the 'right' schools, joining established clubs and political parties, and so on. Unfortunately, this can mean copying not only our best qualities, but also some of our worst. And in the perspective offered by Bateson, newcomers' perceptions and responses to these qualities will be framed within their prior experiences of social differentiation. When social groups interact in this manner, the tenuous boundaries between the ethical and unethical, the criminal and noncriminal, become increasingly blurred. For example, during the lessons many students said television violence, excessive materialism, and the absence of moral education for youth were direct causes of crime. Yet in the received wisdom of Canadian politics and jurisprudence, such ideas would be considered speculative at best, but most importantly unsubstantiated by 'scientific' data. Thus, what one community considers criminal behaviour warranting legal action, another community perceives as conjecture or ambiguity. Within both communities unique experiences of the differentiation of social power have influenced their respective perceptions of the *other*.

The parental wisdom of 'do as I say and not as I do' comes to mind here, particularly for its proven lack of effectiveness. Can we expect newcomers to distinguish easily the nuances between 'unethical' business practices that harm the community and 'clever' business practices that are the exemplars of our entrepreneurial model? Similarly, can we expect altruistic self-restraint when newcomers perceive local elites vigorously exploiting opportunities presented by transitions, technicalities, and ambiguities in public policy? These would seem to be unrealistic expectations even for long-established Canadians. As noted in John Saul's provocative and detailed book, such ambiguities are routinely exploited by our society's 'new generation of owners and managers,' who make little distinction between 'avoiding the letter of the law and evading the law altogether' (Saul 1992, 388). The major problems for newcomers, of course, are when they interpret and extend these 'ambiguous' business practices beyond the generally accepted parameters of the adopted society. Then, the reaction against the 'ungrateful, law-breaking immigrant' can be as strong as it is misdirected.

At the heart of Cooke's quote above is the realization that cultural life, expressed within and through language, comes with 'strings attached.' If we are unable to perceive the unique patterns of our society, it is because we are thoroughly intertwined within the fabric. In the ESL classroom, community development of necessity requires reflection. Teachers should resist defining laws, responsibilities, and community as universal principles exemplified by our perceptions of Canadian society. Instead, we can listen to what our students say and seek out insights about Canadian life that evade our common-sense understanding. If we wish to discourage some newcomers from evaluating citizenship strictly in terms of return on investment, we may need to reflect critically on our own economic attitudes and the conduct of our government in the promotion of our society. If we want newcomers to participate in the collective security of our communities, then we must consider whether newcomers are realistically sharing in the benefits provided by their participation. Such questions and perspectives, uniquely suited for the comparative perspectives of an ESL classroom, provide the necessary foundation for effective community policing.

CHAPTER 6

A Dangerous Future

Introduction

At a past press conference in Toronto to promote a concert, Chrissie Hynde of the rock band the Pretenders was quoted as saying that only men can really rock 'n' roll. To the assembled, it appeared to be an astoundingly sexist remark coming from a most unlikely source: rock music's most prolific and enduring feminist performer. A few media pundits speculated that it wasn't necessarily a compliment. What Hynde had been hinting at was that women didn't really *need* to rock 'n' roll, an art form infamous for its aggression, rebellion, and rage. Hynde was implying that women were more experienced at 'communicating' their personal emotions to each other. In contrast, men are socialized to hide certain emotions and to resist intimacies, particularly with other men. From an early age in our society, masculine identities are often defined in competition with other men, a continual jostling for position in hierarchies of status and power. The tensions that occur from such patterns of socialization find few culturally accepted outlets for expression, one of which is rock music. Chrissie Hynde's comment introduces a central theme for this chapter, one that explores the potential contributions of feminist pedagogy for the ESL classroom and in particular a deeper understanding of sustainable ecological practices. This latter notion and the lessons in this chapter arose one day in response to my students' apprehensions about the environment and, for many, their specific concerns as mothers responding to 'a dangerous future.'

Two important points should be stated right away. First, feminist thought is not a unified or singular approach. Many options and priorities have been put forward under the feminist banner. One set of priorities emphasizes the need to redress the imbalance of power in society: What can be done to help women gain access to privileged positions and salaries? How can our legal, political, and bureaucratic systems be transformed to improve the conditions of women at home, at school, and at work, recognizing the historical inequity of power that has supported predominantly masculine roles and values in powerful institutions? Another set of priorities, one that shall be explored at greater length in this chapter, suggests that feminist practice is not only concerned about equity and access in society, but also with alternative ways of *knowing* and *being* in society and subsequently of reorganizing basic social, economic, and ecological principles. Neither approach excludes the other, and quite often they overlap.[1] Nor should these approaches been seen as exclusive to feminism. Rather, attention to a particular set of concerns reflects historical and political conditions in a given country and the specific imbalances of power that women encounter in terms of race, class, and as immigrants or refugees (see Ng 1989; Goldstein 1994; Peirce 1994, 1995; Rockhill and Tomic 1994). Simply put, there are many ways to experience being a woman. And as noted by Weiler (1991), such realities necessarily create tensions and conflicting political priorities within the feminist movement. Accordingly, she cautions against simplified or essentialized dichotomies when discussing feminine or masculine discourses. Such strategies disguise important differences within feminism and limit the potential for strategic coalitions that feminists might form with other social movements.

The second point to mention is that I write this chapter from the position of an outsider. My experiences at university have taught me that this must be, at best, a partial and second-hand experience and that some feminist writers might feel that my efforts are necessarily doomed to fail before they have begun. Such pessimism is understandable and reflects the contemporary reality that it is both fashionable and politically astute to be seen and heard promoting women's perspectives. Siebers mentions the timeliness and 'tokenism' of some male authors' 'obligatory chapter[s] in support of women's issues' that 'contribute nothing to feminist criticism' (Siebers 1988, 189–190). Other male authors, with impressive critical credentials, espouse feminist positions in a language that is so oppressively abstract and elitist that they end up reinforcing the kinds of social power that exclude women (Yates 1992). Of course, there are two sides to the coin, and some male educators reluctantly resort to tokenism with the knowledge that the mere accusation of sexism is often indefensible and can result in irreparable damage to one's career.

So the question is, why bother? First, I believe that the high quality of the work and the often unique perspectives put forward by feminist researchers warrant serious examination for education. Moreover, in a profession that both advocates for more 'learner-centred' pedagogies and has a predominantly high proportion of female instructors, ignoring or trivializing issues and learning strategies around the notion of gender would contradict the aspirations as well as the demographics of the profession. Second, I believe that to ignore issues of identity around gender, class, race, or sexual orientation in the ESL classroom is the same as saying to our students that they are unimportant (see Vandrick 1997). Fundamental to the politics of education is that when we choose to teach something, and in some special way, we necessarily discard other options. In this way, we unavoidably define what is appropriate and what might be possible in our society. Privileging grammar structures and pronunciation to the exclusion of employment equity or violence against women, for example, has the effect of both denying their relevance to our students' lives and concealing the language resources that are used to either reproduce or remedy such problems. The challenge is to integrate the social and the linguistic together with the possibility that both will be mutually enriched.

Language and Gender

Robin Lakoff has this to say about language and gender:

> Those who have public power thereby have power to make language and make definitions – a power that, in turn, enhances and legitimizes their public power. Men have thus had the unquestioned power and authority to define male and female roles, to control language use, and to legitimize nonlinguistic behavior through that control of language. Since men, in control of the words, are defined as *we*, women become by default *they*. Women are the other, the outsider: unintelligible and therefore not needing to be heard. They are not, literally and figuratively, part of the conversation, the political discourse. (1990, 99)

What does the language of the powerful look and sound like in our society?[2] Many would argue that it is characterized by the appearance of objectivity and scientific analysis. That is, powerful language is dispassionate and distant; it attempts to detach meanings from social contexts of time and place and makes appeals to truth and authority based on principles of formal rationality. Many examples come to mind. Consider the language of the law, the academy, business, government – or even grammar! These are sociolinguistic worlds that have been largely defined, regulated and populated by men. In these areas, language is presented as value-neutral, an instrument of clarity and 'truth.' With skill and refined oratory, *the* truth or *the* main idea of anything can be 'discovered,' lifted from its hiding place. And through the assumed neutrality and control of language, powerful men are able to regulate women's 'non-linguistic' lives.[3]

How can we characterize the language of the 'outsider,' a language that is usually marginalized in terms of decision making in our society? Bordo (in Cherryholmes 1993, 10) offers a description of feminine discourse that she identifies with a 'natural foundation for knowledge, not in detachment and distance, but in closeness, connectedness, and empathy.' In literacy education, a feminist approach to reading and writing would supplement the skills of summarizing, clarifying, and predicting with critical interpretations that explicitly make emotions and personal experiences part of the available *meanings* – no longer singular – produced through texts. And similar to other critical strategies such as poststructuralism, a feminist reading might examine *how* texts are used to reproduce forms of social power: What linguistic resources have been used to present the appearance of detachment, objectivity, and truth? Most importantly, many feminist writers would deny that they were simply producing another analytical framework about language. They would argue that their work, in many fundamental ways, is related to issues of survival and hope in a world of dangerous economic disparities, fragmented societies, nuclear weaponry, and ecological degradation.

A Pedagogical Moment

In the first part of my class, I often ask students if they have heard or seen anything interesting in the news the day before. It is usually an informal situation, arising if other students are arriving late for class. One day in March of 1992, two different news items were mentioned. First, one student spoke about the depletion of the ozone layer and said that parents had been advised not to let their children go out at noon time because of the danger from ultraviolet radiation. Another student then told us about a United Nations report on the AIDS epidemic. She said that it had been described as the fastest growing disease in the world and the largest global health challenge for the future. Alone, either news item would be depressing. But together, the sum of discouragement was greater than its parts. One student from Brazil, a recent mother, said that such news made her wish she didn't have children. This comment unnerved many in the room.

The great majority of my students are women, and for them, having and raising children has been the central concern that defines their identity and often justifies their coming to Canada and leaving the nation of their birth. As well, for many students, having children includes an element of duty mixed in with desire. It is the obligation to one's ancestors to maintain a genealogy of the family name (most often defined as bearing a male 'heir'), and it still remains the most important guarantee of old age social security in most of the world. As evidenced by the class response to the comment from my student from Brazil, for someone to *choose* not to have children appeared so unusual as to be beyond common sense. It was, for all assembled, a profound moment for reflection upon our lives and our futures: an important and un-planned moment to initiate ways of thinking, acting, and making larger connections that are central to a critical ESL pedagogy.

LESSON 1: Speaking activity on 'a dangerous future'
A few minutes after my Brazilian student had spoken, I placed the class in small groups for a speaking activity. The only question that I placed on the board for discussion was, 'Would you ad-vise people against having children in a dangerous future?' The discussions surprised me in a couple of important ways. First, I realized that the form and content of the question offered a degree of flexibility that enabled two different discourses to be interwoven into the activity – one of politics (Why is our future dangerous and what must be done to change it?), the other of the family (What does this mean for my family?). Moreover, by incorporating the function of *advice*, the question also encouraged personal experience for the purpose of political discussion. Sec-ond, what this meant was that several women in my class found themselves discussing 'political' issues, a field of conversation in which they often felt 'incapable' of participating. As well, a couple of men found themselves debating familiar issues, politics and power, on *unfamiliar* terms and with previously reticent partners. On a couple of occasions, I made the point of mentioning this observation to the small groups for their reflection.

Teacher's Note: This last intervention on my part requires some the-oretical elaboration. In critical pedagogy, affirming students' personal experiences and forms of knowledge are important.[4] *Such encourage-ment, however, should not come at the loss of critically evaluating these same experiences (Simon 1992, 24). In the above lesson, I made space in the class to articulate the kinds of linguistic and emotional responses about our future that, as noted by Lakoff, would be excluded from a 'serious' (i.e., masculine) discussion on political solutions. At the same time, by pointing out the contributions of previously silent students, predominantly women, I was encouraging critical reflection on how or why some students had previously felt 'incapable' of participating in this type of discussion. This example of 'problem-posing' was an opportunity for students to consider their personal feelings of inadequacy as socially produced, as products of discourses that actively discourage alternative knowledge forms.*

As mentioned earlier, discourses police themselves in very important and powerful ways. If you want to be heard – to be 'intelligible' – in a discourse, and you want to challenge or critique something in a discourse, you must often learn and use its specific language forms and vocabulary. Once you overcome this initial hurdle, however, your critique can become either effectively neutralized or compromised. By neutralized, I mean that the language one must use to converse with 'peers' is a language that inherently controls serious critique of the underlying social interests and inequalities that the discourse helps perpetuate.[5] In terms of compromise, I wish to point out that any specialized language (e.g., financial, academic, political) takes a lot of time, energy, and often money, to acquire. Therefore, people have strong interests vested in the continued prestige and exclusiveness of the discourses they have acquired.

In the lesson above, talking about the importance of children in a dangerous future is to begin critical work from a place of experience familiar to many students. It means affirming and valuing these experiences, but also critically evaluating how they are socially constructed. Many important questions can then be integrated into the classroom activity: Why do some people feel that their experiences of nurturing and homemaking necessarily exclude them from participating in public-policy decisions? Whose interests are served by defining these experiences as irrelevant? Such questions offer perspectives that are essential to initiate the kinds of profound and necessary political alternatives that feminist authors advocate.

Compositions

After about an hour, we broke up the small groups and then collectively talked about important ideas and comments from the earlier discussion. I mentioned that this might make a good topic for our book, *Stories from Our Class* (see Morgan 1992). Several students chose this discussion for their compositions. I have included a few of them as they appeared in our book, with structural corrections included. Of note, both compositions display extensive use of correlative conjunctions (e.g., both/and, not only/ but also, either/or, neither/nor), which I had introduced to assist in their writing around this time, particularly for Lesson 2 in this chapter.

> Neither men nor women deny the value of children for the future of our society. Today we are not only enjoying the fruits of high technology but also suffering their effects. Even though science is advanced, we still have many man-made problems with nature. Some of the natural environment has been damaged by people. Also people have suffered from new diseases. The more we explore the mysteries, the more we become afraid of facing our unknown future.
>
> Evading a dangerous future is impossible unless you don't have any children. Parents who have accepted more education have already recognized that the future is the most important thing for their children. They also know their children will live in a more dangerous world if we don't improve our environment now. So, we are not only worrying about the upbringing of children, but also their development in the future. Therefore, if a couple decides to get married, they will plan not only for themselves, but also about having children or not. But I believe people's decision making is influenced by many factors such as culture, education, and religion. For example, when the Persian Gulf war ended, many babies were born among army families. This may be one of many factors to change their mind.
>
> Of course, if you don't have children, you won't worry about anything in the future. In contrast, we should teach our children

how to face a dangerous future, to understand how to protect our environment, and to avoid the same mistakes as ours. The above problems are the most difficult tasks which will take a long time to fight. So we are looking forward to our children working it out.

In my experience, if a married couple doesn't have children after a few years, they will be very lonely when they get older.

In older traditions, if people didn't have children within a few years of marriage, the women would get a lot of complaints, either from the in-laws or husbands. The Chinese have an idiom, 'Save food stuffs for the famine, and raise children for protection in old age.' In older people's minds, boys are more important than girls because when children grow up, parents always depend on the boys. The girls do not belong to the parents after they get married.

Times have changed and most people are concerned about a lot of things. Before they have a baby, they think about not only economic problems, but also the time schedules. For example, they must have enough spare time to take care of a child. So, in a dangerous future, I'll advise people not to have many children; but at least have one. If everybody were scared about a dangerous future and refused to have children, the world would end and there would be no young people to develop the future.

LESSON 2: Critical literacy/Reading two texts about ozone depletion

Using 'parallel' articles on the same subject can be a useful teaching device to facilitate critical language awareness (CLA) (see Clark et al. 1990, 1991; Corson 1993; Fairclough 1992; Janks 1993; Morgan 1996a). Within this area of language study, critical linguistics and critical discourse analysis (CDA) (Kress 1991; Lemke 1989; Wodak 1990) are particularly focused on the structural and lexical features of language that can be used to reproduce or challenge social authority. The choice of these two articles and the reading strategies I incorporated were based upon my interests in CLA and CDA, as well as many of the ideas raised in Lesson 1. First, I wanted to reemphasize the point that individual feelings of 'inadequacy' are often effects of language and that texts such as newspaper articles are constructed to produce specific meanings and sometimes silence alternative readings, particularly when such readings pertain to contentious social issues, such as responsibility for environmental destruction. By comparing two articles on the same subject, readers are better able to recognize the particular 'hidden agenda' that is inscribed within either or both texts. As well, students can become adept at using similar language resources to represent their own interests when necessary.

Students already have some notion of this idea – a recognition of ideological coercion – in their own language and country. It is important, however, to remember that each country provides a different set of sociocultural contexts and conditions that make one text more persuasive or more authoritative than others. That is, a text is constructed as if it was engaged in a localized dialogue, an 'intertextuality' (see Lemke 1989; Halliday and Hasan 1985) with past and current texts within a community or society. This dialogue may be complementary or competitive. A text has a *voice*; it assembles a set of structures and vocabulary to reflect favourably on the social interests of the authors and project negative motives upon opposing social interests. A text, then, becomes a *context* for other texts that later respond to its assertions.

The key point is that articles usually want to do something – convince the reader to act or to remain acquiescent. But in order to do this, an author must abide by certain codes and conventions of time and place.[6] For example, in our society, articles that *appear* to be reporting, describing, or documenting 'facts' are held to be more 'truthful' than personalized, emotional, or interpretational texts (Lemke 1989). Moreover, powerful groups and institutions that act upon 'scientific' facts are given greater support and receive less opposition. In our society, therefore, the impression of 'objectivity' is as powerful as any reality, and the language resources that are employed to construct this impression are as political as any ballot box in an election. In order to make informed and fair decisions about public life, such language activities need to be made discernable and explicit for all.

The second perspective I wanted to introduce in this lesson pertained to the types of concerns raised by feminist writers in terms of both literacy skills and environmental awareness. As mentioned earlier (Bordo cited in Cherryholmes 1993, 10), such a reading would seek to produce knowledge based not on 'detachment and distance, but on closeness, connectedness, and empathy.' A feminist reading, in this perspective, would link analytical with emotional meanings and literacy skills, viewing their prior separation in the the context of gendered power, and promoting their integration as a necessary precondition for social and ecological sustainability. As well, a feminist reading might use parallel texts to illustrate how discursive strategies and 'contradictions' are used to forward a particular political agenda. In the classroom, for example, we might try to learn how certain texts speak directly to readers' emotions, controlling potentially dangerous and subversive feelings through the authority of ostensibly 'unemotional' or 'factual' language.

Reading

The first article we read came from the *Toronto Star* and was entitled, 'Sun-risk warnings begin next month (1992, A5).' The article sets out to explain why too much sun exposure is dangerous (ultraviolet radiation) and explains how the ozone layer is being damaged by certain chemicals such as CFCs. Also, the article includes a public statement from the environmental group Greenpeace, which calls on the Canadian government to make immediate bans of ozone-damaging chemicals. Prior to reading the article, we reviewed ideas from Lesson 1. Each student read the article silently. We then took up the article as a group with each student reading a passage out loud followed by clarification of any vocabulary, pronunciation, and structural problems that occurred. Students were then placed in groups to discuss the following questions:

1) What is the ozone layer?
2) What causes ozone depletion?
3) Is Greenpeace satisfied with the government's action?
4) Will you change your lifestyle (sun habits) after reading this article?
5) How do you feel about the future after reading this article?

The first three questions were designed specifically to evaluate a 'functional' level of literacy. Questions #4 and #5, in contrast, are intended to generate experiential and emotional meanings in the reading. The discussion of #4 and #5, similar to Lesson 1, indicated a deep concern for the present and future safety of children around sun exposure. Interestingly, most of my Asian students had always avoided the sun because they considered suntans unattractive and characteristic of subordinate social classes. In contrast, my students from Brazil and Europe saw this article as posing a serious threat to lifestyle and cultural conceptions of beauty. Several of them spoke about the importance of using sun block, hats, and protective clothing for themselves and children. The general consensus of the class was that this was a depressing article.

My next strategy was to get the class involved in the type of textual analyses inspired by writers in critical discourse analysis. I asked the students one last question and wrote it on the board:

6) Which words, sentences, and ideas in the article made you feel worried, depressed, or angry?

Most students found the word 'warning' of particular concern, noting its presence in the title and in several paragraphs. Indeed, the second paragraph is a single sentence, which reads: 'The warnings will begin a year earlier than expected.' This latter urgency in time was also of concern. A reference to 'skin cancer' was raised. Another area of the article mentioned by students comes from quotes attributed to a spokesperson from Greenpeace: I don't think it's great that we're getting daily warnings. I think it's sad.' Also, 'We can't hide from the effects of ozone depletion by staying inside ... let's not forget that there are going to be effects on crops, marine life – in fact, on all life.' As pointed out by the class, these latter comments from Greenpeace not only raised anxiety, but also focused accountability for the situation, and that responsibility was being directed at the Canadian government. Question #6, coming as it did after #5, interconnected emotional and analytical literacy skills, encouraging both a kind of critical distance and a recognition that 'feelings' were meanings evoked and potentially exploited through texts.

The second article we read came from *Time* magazine and was entitled 'Hats On!' (1992, 42). The title of the article provides a good indication of its focus, which was on ways to protect oneself in the sun. The article has a completely different tone about the seriousness of the situation, however. For example, the first sentence of the article states, 'Ozone depletion is cause for caution, but it's no reason to stay barricaded indoors or put on an astronaut suit before venturing outside.' Similarly, an 'expert' from NASA is cited to add authority to the relaxed sensibility of the piece: 'We're not talking about a single exposure to a death ray. It takes repeated exposure over long periods of times.'

We followed the same reading procedure as the first article. After having read the prior piece the day before, the focus of the questions became comparative as well as singularly focused. For example, instead of asking the students how they felt after reading the article, I asked them how they felt in comparison to the previous article. Also, after having separated questions #5 and #6 in the previous reading activity, this was no longer possible or desirable during the activities around the *Time* magazine piece. Students were linking feelings and specific language devices together in their discussions on the text. For example, one student noted that the following sentence made her feel that the ozone problem wasn't serious because of the adverbial of time 'always': 'Excessive exposure to the sun's ultraviolet (UV) rays has always been dangerous.' I also pointed out how the verb tense selected (present perfect) emphasized this 'forever' notion by its function of suggesting continuity of an action or situation from the past into the present. The following sentences received particular attention from many students: 'Even if there were no atmospheric damage, an estimated one-sixth of all Americans, for example, would still develop skin cancer during their lifetime. Most cases are curable, if detected early.' These sentences suggested 'no problem' to the students and presented a view of the seriousness of ozone depletion in large variance to the *Toronto Star* piece. In the conditional sentence, we noted the extra emphases provided by 'even if' and 'still' which further suggested the inevitability and 'naturalness' of skin cancer.

The examples mentioned were important because they provided insights into grammar structure that are rarely considered in the ESL classroom. As emphasized by researchers in critical discourse analysis, parts of speech and vocabulary do not simply represent or transmit a fixed reality. In fact, they *project* a sense of reality that is very much an effect of the language resources that have been used (see Kress 1991). That is, if I want to tell people not to worry about something, like the author of the *Time* magazine piece, I will *use* structures and other language resources that produce a feeling that 'this has always been a natural part of life and it will always be so.' Moreover, I might write this way with an understanding that some readers who are *critically* illiterate would assume that my choice of structures and vocabulary meant that I was *reporting* something rather than *interpreting* it or concealing other possible meanings.[7]

Our next focus, was on what I would call the 'contradictions' produced by the texts and how the use of parallel texts on the same subject helped us to 'read' them. The first key point to make had already been experienced and discussed by the class. Both articles were on the same topic, the consequences and effects of ozone depletion. But both articles offered different estimations of the seriousness of the problem, an emotionally charged problem that directly touched who we are and who we might become: 'Is it safe or not safe to bring children into the world?' The second point to make, a key one for a critical and feminist reading, was how did these two meanings *contradict* the language that 'described' the situation? That is, although both articles talked authoritatively as if they were reporting the 'truth' – a discourse strategy produced through detached and objective language forms – in reality they were *interpreting* the situation – offering opinions. Otherwise, they would both have the same meanings, or evoke the same emotions from the students in the class.

To highlight this contradiction, I asked a couple of questions to generate discussion. First, as an example of problem-posing, I asked the class who the authors of the articles were, although no authors are credited in either piece. We then talked about when authors are mentioned or anonymous in articles and what kinds of effects on meanings are a result. Most of us felt that when no author is specified, we are more likely to believe that we are reading a report or description of events instead of an opinion. I followed up this idea by asking students about the kinds of pronouns, adverbials, and other language items we might use to show opinions. We noted that lexical items and grammar forms that signify opinions, interpretations, or qualifications (e.g., first-person pronouns, adverbials of possibility) are absent in the articles, with the exception of the statements from experts placed within quotation marks. Thus the students and I felt that the 'appearance' of these texts contradicted their intentions and effects on my students. Moreover, we speculated on the social interests and social privileges that would be promoted by such language strategies (see student composition below).

As a language teacher, my objectives were not so much in assigning right and wrong, adjudicating between the *Toronto Star* and *Time* magazine, but rather providing critical insights into language use. In the context of this lesson, this also included concerns and reading strategies raised by feminist authors such as Lakoff and Bordo. In a very practical and classroom-focused way, I was interested in examining how, in Lakoff's perspective, powerful individuals are able 'to control language use, and to legitimize nonlinguistic behaviour through that control of language.' How did both texts potentially diminish ways of knowing that emphasized connectedness, empathy, and personal politics? In our classroom activities, we gained a better sense of how texts control or manage 'dangerous' emotions by appearing unemotional or scientific, talking about the 'facts' in a factual language that some women are often excluded from in their day-to-day lives. To stop our reading and our analysis here would be unsatisfactory, however. The goal for a critical educator, I suggest, is to offer students *many* ways of reading – critically, emotionally, functionally – in order that they might become less 'naive' readers and more able to read a number of possible social meanings and consequences that a text poses for their community. In this way, personal meanings can become both political and ethical, and provide important support for community mobilization and activism (see Cherryholmes 1993).

Student Writing

The following article comes from *Stories from Our Class* and was written after our lessons using parallel texts. I feel that this composition exemplifies the connectedness of experiential and critical readings that was the intention of the classroom activities. Personal experiences, memories, and emotions are brought to bear, or to make meanings *within, against,* and *upon* contemporary texts and subsequently to inform others and direct actions for the possible benefit of the community (see Cherryholmes 1993; Scholes 1985).

> The articles awakened reminiscences of my youth. I started reading newspapers and magazines shortly after Japan invaded China's northeastern provinces in 1931. This tragic event strengthened Chinese Nationalism to an unprecedented height. Chinese publications in Shanghai called on Chinese youth everyday to pay more attention to the national crisis and get ready for any eventualities. Politicians predicted that a life and death struggle was inevitable.
>
> Many booklets came out from the press indoctrinating students and young people about how to recognize the true situation. I remember there was a booklet which was entitled 'How to read news and not be fooled by it.' It was an enlightening book. It named all the important news agencies of the world and analysed them about their backgrounds, what people they served and what were their interests. Armed with such understanding we would not be fooled by propaganda.
>
> During the thirties, Chinese newspapers reported a news item sometimes with more than two agencies' reports. This was a laudable practice. Readers could get the most reliable news out of it by comparison.

I read two articles recently. Both of them discussed a similar problem, the depletion of the ozone layers. One article was published by Canada Press, the other by *Time* magazine. They took a diametrically opposed attitude toward this problem. The CP article paid much concern not only to human life, but also to the life of other living things which we need for our daily life and urged our government to halve the production of CFCs as soon as possible.

Time's article played down the seriousness of the problem by saying that the UV rays have always been dangerous; the depletion of ozone layer just added to the risk. It means this is an old problem, not a new one. We should not get into a great fuss. It made some suggestions for protection, but the suggestions are only applicable to human beings and not to other things.

Time is an American magazine. It represents American interests and speaks for her. It is understood without saying that the U.S.A. is the number one country which makes the most pollution and depletion of the ozone layer in the world. The reason it didn't want to explain this matter was to avoid any further embarrassment.

Now, let me quote a Chinese folktale to end this writing:

Once upon a time, there was a boy of a landlord's family who broke the head of his playmate unintentionally. Blood came out slowly. The wounded boy cried and ran home to his mother. His mother brought him to the landlord's and complained about the mishap to him. The landlord was surprised at first and then said, 'Let me see the wound, I found out that the crack is an old one, not a new one. My son had nothing to do with it. You'd better go home and keep quiet or else.' The woman cried and left with her grievances. News spread out. Everybody in the neighbourhood heard it but no one dared to say anything.

Is there any similarity between the landlord and our powerful neighbour in the south?

Follow-up readings

On 12 March 1992, an article appeared in the *Toronto Star* (A10) entitled 'U.S. risks world's future, Strong says.' The last composition by my student above had indeed been prescient in its observations about our 'powerful neighbour to the south.' The article extensively quoted the concerns of Maurice Strong, who was at the time the secretary-general of the United Nations Earth Summit, later held in Rio de Janeiro. Two pre-reading questions for group discussion were designed to link this article explicitly to the earlier activities: 1) What do you remember about the two stories we read about ozone depletion? 2) How did you feel after reading them?

The article provided many powerful criticisms and practical ideas. In particular, Strong singled out the low cost of American energy as a prime cause of excessive pollution and pointed out that countries with higher energy costs (e.g., Japan and Germany) had stronger economies because of incentives to improve their production by developing innovative technologies to conserve energy. We learnt some interesting vocabulary from the article, such as 'environmental aggression' and 'widespread extinction of species.' In general, the article was well-received by the class because it showed that some people in positions of authority were speaking out about the environment and offering tangible solutions for problems.

On 7 April 1992, the *Toronto Star* (A3) published an article entitled '2 top Bata executives fined for polluting.' The article discussed a 'precedent-setting judgement' that made executives personally accountable for pollution caused by a company. The court's decision was unique in other ways. The company was ordered not to pay the $12,000 fines assessed the executives and the company itself was ordered to pay $120,000 in fines. As well, the court ordered the company to pay half of its fine to a local community group that fights pollution and promotes recycling. This article was very popular with the class. The idea of holding executives accountable for the environmental destruction caused by their companies was unanimously supported.

These last two articles were important in another aspect relevant to the priorities of a critical ESL pedagogy. It has been my intention in this chapter to go beyond the sometimes trivial and superficial ways in which experience is addressed in the ESL classroom. And to undertake this type of practice, I believe an important condition needs to be included. If we are to utilize alternative ways of knowing, being, and learning, in support of our social and environmental concerns, we should try to offer examples of possibility and hope whenever and wherever they may occur. When people perceive a 'dangerous future' as a matter of fate, of natural evolution, and beyond their 'minuscule' influence, then they will surely resign themselves to passivity and the worst that fate delivers. When small victories and dissenting voices are discerned, as in the two latter readings, alternative and sustainable ways of community life have the real possibility of developing.

Conclusion

Throughout history, men have been socialized to manage both the positions and procedures of social power. But not all men have attained such privileges. History has also shown that powerful men have consistently demonstrated a capacity to differentiate themselves from and oppress other men as well as women, and they have done this based on real and invented categorizations of race, class, and ethnicity. So, when we talk about patriarchal authority, we are not speaking about biological or natural propensities. Rather, we are speaking about complex interrelationships of time and place that define both gender roles and authority. The challenge for feminist pedagogies is to make connections between gender, race, class, and history that are appropriate to the particular social contexts where pedagogy is intended to take effect. Otherwise, change may be superficial at best. At worst is the possibility that women simply change places with powerful men only to perpetuate oppressive practices that preceded them.

It is precisely because social norms and language practices are internalized and taken for granted that those who use them habitually are unable or unwilling to recognize their adverse consequences in the short and long terms. And it is because women have been largely outsiders in the implementation of power that feminist pedagogies can offer unique and necessary perspectives on the consequences of dangerous forms of decision-making.

Throughout modern Western civilization, what we call the scientific method has commanded obedience in most facets of our lives. It is a way of thinking and organizing that has produced incredible technological achievements, but by the same procedures has also fragmented and alienated social life, poisoned much of our environment, and severely limited the types of responses that are necessary to resolve these problems. Many feminists and ecologists converge in their analyses of the situation and their suggestions for alternative ways of living. They propose the concept of 'ecofeminism' (Plant 1990, 79), for example, as a way of 'thinking feelingly' about our world and our relations to it.

As proposed by ecofeminists, we need to look both emotionally and intellectually at all aspects of our social world in order to live responsibly. To this end, language is a central concern and important site of transformation. The language we use, and the ways that we teach it or organize it, help define our relations to our environment and other species in the world. Science, it should be remembered, is not only a set a techniques, but also a configuration of reinforcing language practices (Lemke 1987). Mechanistic notions of language support mechanistic relationships with our environment. As has been the case since the Industrial Revolution, the environment is then rendered conceptually separate from human activity, something to control, dominate, and exploit in the name of economic 'progress.' In contrast, it is often when we give 'voices' – the equivalent language of human interaction – to the various species of the world that we place ourselves in a relationship of connectedness, interdependence, and respect. This notion seems to have been largely lost on Western civilization, although it still remains an important feature of aboriginal peoples, whose traditional economies required a comprehensive understanding of ecology for survival (see Morgan 1991).

The ESL classroom is a relevant place to explore issues and interconnections about the environment, feminist pedagogies, and critical language awareness. At the same time, I would caution against approaching these notions as merely topics or themes to facilitate more effective L2 acquisition. I believe that we need to scrape below the surface of many of our cherished concepts and assumptions about language if we want to approach ecofeminist principles in a genuinely transformative way. Indeed, we may find forms of patriarchal authority rather close to home, and we might have to consider ecology not as 'outside' of language, but as intrinsic to it, if we are to live responsibly in a dangerous future.

In Closing

Introduction

I remember the first time I presented some of the lesson plans from this book at an ESL conference. I was part of a panel presentation that began with an introductory discussion on the importance of an understanding of language and power issues for the ESL classroom. Early on, a couple of audience members voiced their scepticism about the relevance of our focus. They said that our work was 'too theoretical' or 'too academic' to be of any practical use. When my segment of the presentation was discussed, the responses tended towards extremes. Some teachers wanted to explore relationships of language and power in their classroom but weren't sure how to go about it while maintaining familiar concerns about speaking, listening, reading, and writing. Many of these teachers enthusiastically approached me afterwards for copies of my lesson plans and with requests for more 'practical' materials. In contrast, others in attendance were quite put off by the subject material and felt that the lesson plans were a bit disjointed as a result: 'It's very interesting, but it's not ESL.' If there was a common thread running through both responses, it was the challenge of demonstrating the usefulness of these lessons to as wide a group of ESL teachers as possible.

A Challenge for Theorists

This book has been conceptualized largely as a result of the types of varied objections and interests raised above. In part, I was

motivated to write a book that questioned some of the fundamental beliefs of my colleagues at the university, both of critical persuasion and otherwise. In particular, I wanted to echo
the concerns raised by several authors (Clarke 1993; Pennycook
1989; Giroux 1994; Morgan 1997a; van Lier 1994) regarding the
disproportionate influence of theory over practice that prevails in
ESL and education in general. My teaching experiences in Canada
and abroad have frequently demonstrated to me that the knowledge forms produced at the university are far less essential or
generalizable than assumed. The origins of this book serve as an
important example. Many of my ideas and lessons were inspired
by colleagues at the community centre where I worked after I
came back from China. Although they hadn't read about poststructuralism or critical pedagogy, their classes *already* addressed
many of the social and language issues featured in this book.
Clearly, they were actively and intuitively 'theorizing' on the
day-to-day conditions of their practice. What they didn't *have* –
rather than *lacked* – was the formal, descriptive code of theory,
sanctioned by the university and conferring status and power in
both the discipline and in local ESL bureaucracies.

My colleagues at the community centre didn't see their work as
'outside' of ESL or at the sacrifice of other priorities. They simply
didn't feel that it was necessary to follow the various orthodox-
ies emanating from professional language journals. In their reading habits they tended to avoid, along with critical theories, the
'latest' research on second language acquisition, communicative
approaches, learner-centred approaches, action research, and so
on. Many of them liked to do repetitive drills. Some allowed a lot
of L1 spoken in the classroom. They believed that certain social
and community concerns often needed development in the first
language prior to meaningful use in a second or third (see Auerbach 1993; Faltis and Hudelson 1994; Lucas and Katz 1994; Morgan 1996b). Others, upon request from students, taught explicit
grammar structures. Circumstances allowed and required my colleagues to trust the judgement of their students over the advice
of 'experts.' The program and their jobs survived only through
continued attendance from students and an adventurous syllabus,
of their own making, that directly and immediately satisfied the

expectations and experiences of their students. Of course, some students didn't like the program and went elsewhere. But many came, and many more were attracted to the program through the growing reputation of the centre and the recommendation of friends.

The key point that I address to my colleagues at the university is that the community centre was not and is not dependent on them in order to provide effective and successful language programs. Teachers in these environments have their own unique experiences and forms of expertise that cannot be duplicated in the laboratory-like conditions of the academy. If theoretical knowledge is to be relevant, it must begin by negotiation and a considerable amount of local autonomy. This would require, of course, a relationship of equality between theorist and classroom teacher. In reference to my conference presentation above, equal footing for negotiation should begin with a recognition that the debate about what is or is not ESL usually takes place without those who *do* ESL on a regular basis. Most ESL teachers, in my experience, stay away from conferences. They can't afford the fees and some employers, many of whom serve as organizers of conferences, deny teachers paid professional development that would encourage negotiation and equality. If theorists and academics want to engage in a meaningful exchange with practitioners, they should also consider exploring a whole range of labour related issues that might appear extraneous to language but, I would argue, determine the conditions in which successful language learning can take place.

A Challenge for Practitioners

The main purpose for this book is to encourage teachers and provide them with an opportunity to explore critical perspectives in their classrooms. I do not see these lessons as replacing other more 'traditional' concerns, but rather as a complement to existing practices. At the same time, I have argued throughout this book that these types of lessons should not be considered marginal or secondary to the 'foundations' of language learning. These lessons emerged and were successful because they reflected the immediate and localized *social* concerns of my students. Accordingly, they may be more appropriate in some programs and less in others. For teachers this means that they will probably have to improvise or transpose these lessons to correspond to the administrative constraints of their program and the expectations and experiences of their students. But this would be an important precondition for all lesson planning.

The key point for teachers here is that they have to take responsibility for their own practice. I hope that teachers who read this book will always look critically and creatively at what is or is not ESL. When 'top-down' decisions are being made regarding the 'priorities' of the syllabus, I hope that they will be able to speak forcefully on behalf of their students and their own experiences and intuitions. I believe that it is essential in this regard for classroom teachers to become theoretically aware and theoretically engaged in what happens at the university. There are two important reasons for this. One, universities remain one of the rare social places where useful and challenging ideas, from a broad disciplinary spectrum, are given sufficient time and resources to develop. From firsthand experience, I can say that these ideas can have a profound influence on providing meaningful instruction for students. Not to be forgotten, new ideas can also make teaching interesting and exciting in spite of the familiarity of the surroundings.

The second reason for a teacher's theoretical awareness pertains to the issue of decision-making and power. Most classroom teachers toil at the bottom of the hierarchy of the ESL profession. They are rarely consulted or only in superficial ways that appear consultative. As mentioned throughout this book, the language of power in ESL is theoretical language. Teachers are often confronted with the 'latest' research from an ESL journal as if it were an unassailable 'truth.' This is never the case. No theory in language has emerged without a subsequent theory that challenges or questions some of its major assertions. If teachers want to further their own interests in regards to their conditions of work, they will have to learn to recognize when theory is used as a weapon to promote interests that have little to do with language learning. And to counter such uses effectively, teachers will need to learn more about the 'discourse' of ESL: the rules and codes that govern what and who can speak with authority. Teachers will need to know the competing citations and qualifications that challenge the power of the 'latest' research. Moreover, teachers might consider challenging the discourse of ESL on its own terms: alternative conferences that include a wide range of issues particular to the working conditions of teachers and the social conditions of students; also, ESL teacher's journals that do the same.

What's Next?

I can't overemphasize the fact that these lessons emerged from a set of social and administrative conditions that encouraged flexibility and autonomy at the classroom level. My concern is that these necessary conditions, and subsequently this kind of teaching, are currently in danger of disappearing. In particular, the kinds of critical approaches I advocate for in this book are vulnerable to political and financial pressures for greater standardization in curricula. Once again, schools have emerged as the favourite and most convenient excuse for the recent failures of our economic and political elites. Certain standards or benchmarks are not necessarily bad or undesirable. But what often happens in times of social and economic decline is that standards can serve as forms of surveillance that *produce* examples of educational failure rather than discover them (see Cummins and Cameron 1994). Media that represent elite interests then seize upon such examples to demand changes that detract attention from underlying inequalities more pertinent to the national and global problems we face.

The emerging concerns for ESL and for the ideas in this book revolve around current pressures to make classes conform to national or regional standards at the sacrifice of unique and incommensurable local concerns and responses. If there are to be standards, how much autonomy will be granted to local programs in order to maintain needed funding? Standards tied to funding often mean fixed periods of instruction and a 'core' curriculum within this restricted time frame. 'Alternative' curricula, regardless of their popularity with students and teachers, are certain to be sacrificed. Moreover, teachers are likely to become de-skilled as a result. The importance of responding to the particular experiences of students will be subordinated to the need of getting them through the standardized tests at risk of losing one's job. The long-term results will be reflected in lower pay and fewer benefits befitting a down-graded job that requires minimal skills. Where will the 'expertise' and subsequent funding be concentrated in such a situation? My recent experiences suggest that this type of expertise will come exclusively from the universities where research paradigms are particularly suited to the generalization of hypotheses hatched from often isolated and controlled environments.

Another issue in the standardization debate is over who should speak on behalf of teachers and students. This role is likely to be taken up by professional associations that claim to represent the interests of ESL teachers. One of the difficulties in this situation is that most of the individuals who volunteer their time and considerable energy as executives in these associations come from ESL management or the academic establishment. Regardless of their dedication and best intentions, most of those negotiating on behalf of the profession are largely immune from the adverse consequences of standardized curricula, professional credentials, and stricter top-down control. Indeed, they are the most likely to benefit as academic consultants are increasingly called upon to provide a stamp of theoretical legitimacy for budget-slashing governments.

I suspect that the next few years will be difficult ones for ESL. Both theorists and practitioners have important interests in common in the continued strength and promotion of the profession. I hope that those who are asked to negotiate on behalf of teachers and students take into careful account both the strengths and the limitations of their experiences and expand their consultations accordingly. And in the spirit of this book, I hope that teachers actively and *critically* participate in the decisions that are certain to effect their professional lives and the relationships they have with their students.

APPENDIX ONE

From *Teaching the Gulf War in an ESL Classroom* by Brian Morgan

JINGOISM
Mad dogs and Englishmen

*The following terms have all been used by the British press
to report on the war in the Persian Gulf*

By *The Guardian Weekly*

They have	We have
A war machine	Army, Navy and Air Force
Censorship	Reporting guidelines
Propaganda	Press briefings

They	We
Destroy	Take out
Destroy	Suppress
Kill	Eliminate
Kill	Neutralize
Kill	Decapitate
Cower in foxholes	Dig in

They launch	We launch
Sneak missile attacks	First strikes
Without provocation	Pre-emptively

Their men are...	Our men are...
Troops	Boys
Hordes	Lads

They are...	Our boys are...
Brainwashed	Professional
Paper tigers	Lionhearted
Cowardly	Cautious

Desperate	Confident
Cornered	Heroes
Cannon fodder	Dare devils
Bastards of Baghdad	Young knights of the skies
Blindly obedient	Loyal
Mad dogs	Desert rats
Ruthless	Resolute
Fanatical	Brave

Their boys are motivated by
Fear of Saddam

Our boys are motivated by
Old-fashioned sense of duty

Their boys
Cower in concrete bunkers

Our boys
Fly into the jaws of hell

Iraq ships are
A navy

Our ships are
An armada

Iraqi non-retaliation is
Blundering/Cowardly

Israeli non-retaliation is
An act of great statesmanship

Their missiles are...
Aging duds (rhymes with Scuds)

Our missiles are...
Like Luke Skywalker zapping Darth
Vader

Their missiles cause...
Civilian casualties

Our missiles cause...
Collateral damage

They...
Fire wildly at anything

We...
Precision bomb

Their PoWs are...
Overgrown schoolchildren

Our PoWs are...
Gallant boys

Saddam Hussein is...
Demented
Defiant
An evil tyrant
A crackpot monster

George Bush is...
At peace with himself
Resolute
Statesmanlike
Assured

Their planes...	Our planes...
Are shot out of the sky	Suffer a high rate of attrition
Are zapped	Fail to return from missions

Appendix reprinted from the *Globe and Mail* (23 February 1991, D5)

APPENDIX TWO

Assignment

A word, like a good bowl of soup or stew, has many flavours (meanings) inside. The many meanings and uses for a single word influence other words nearby. It then becomes impossible to remove or separate these 'spices' from each other. That is, although you have ordered something called beef stew, it is impossible to remove the salt, pepper, vinegar, meat, etc., from within it. They have all combined to form a general impression that you like or you don't like. Similarly, when you choose a word to describe a situation, it is difficult for the reader or listener to ignore the other meanings that are familiar to the word's usage. Of course, this coincidence of meanings can be accidental or intentional. In fact, it is also a very powerful, but disguised, form of persuasion in our society.

In your group, explore these examples:

Word	Meaning(s)	Uses/Contexts	Feelings: +/-/n
1) Horde			
2) Lads			
3) To destroy			
4) To neutralize			
5) Cowardly			
6) Cautious			
7) Defiant			
8) Resolute			

Notes

1. The communicative approach has gained a prominent place in language teaching. Although different versions and emphases of this approach exist, a key distinction from earlier methods was the importance of real and meaningful language situations to encourage language learning (see Brumfit and Johnson 1979; Canale and Swain 1980; Swain 1984). Ironically, in my own training, which I suspect was duplicated in other grammar-centred language programs, 'communicative' approaches functioned almost exclusively to accelerate the acquisition of discrete structural items rather than explore 'real' language situations.

   In my training, as well, this strategy was influenced by Chomsky's transformational grammar and his persuasive notion of an internalized 'language acquisition device.' Thus, 'communicative' activities functioned primarily as a necessary experiential component with which an innate, general linguistic capacity is channeled towards a specific grammatical comprehension – from a 'universal grammar' to a 'particular mental grammar' (Botha 1989, 26).

   Arguments for or against Chomsky's linguistics are beyond the scope of this book, particularly considering that Chomsky discourages pedagogical applications for his work. What I find more interesting are the effects his theories have had on the teaching profession, because of the 'scientific' claims he makes based upon his research methods. To claim science as the foundation of one's work is to construct a powerful *social* truth, a discursive truth (see Note 3 below), which commands resources and attention often to the exclusion of other knowledge claims. Regardless of Chomsky's disavowal, we live in a particular sociohistorical period that compels

ESL researchers to examine and privilege scientific-empirical research on
language. To do otherwise would be deemed *socially* irresponsible.

2. Poststructuralism is a fascinating and often difficult area of theory.
It can best be described in relation to some of the ideas that define
structuralism. Structuralism is a way of understanding things based
upon their interrelationships within certain systems or *structures*, not
as isolated phenomena. For example, a structuralist perspective might
generate insights about a religious system or a kinship system by studying
how they articulate to the mode of economy in the particular society being
observed (see Kuper 1973; Sahlins 1972).

Much of this line of thinking is indebted to the thought of Ferdinand
de Saussure, whose work on structural linguistics provides a starting
point for poststructural ideas on the relationships of language, society,
and power. Saussure talks about language as a *signifying* system made
up of linguistic signs. He points out that a linguistic sign (a word in
English, for example) carries no intrinsic correspondence to the meaning
associated with it. There is no innate reason that the sound uttered to
make *dog* is a natural correspondence to the image or concept. Saussure
describes two components that form and enable the functioning of a sign:
a *signifier*, such as a sound or graphic image; and the *signified*, the concept
or image to which it refers. Signs are 'arbitrary' social constructions,
hence the sign *chien* in French or *Hund* in German in place of the English
term.

Moreover, Saussure recognizes that signs have meanings based upon
their differences from other signs *within* a particular language. For example,
the sign 'umbrella' in English often functions in current usage where two
signs – *Regenschirm* ('rain protector') and *Sonnenschirm* ('sun protector')
– function in German. As one sign shifts along a 'chain of meaning,'
others do as well. In English, for example, signs such as 'communism' and
'socialism' have meanings based upon the shifting meanings associated
with capitalism.

Whereas structural linguistics identifies differences within signifying
systems, poststructuralism asks probing questions about how, why,
and in whose interests such 'meaning' differences take place; whereas
structuralism concentrates on ahistorical or synchronic analyses of language
systems, poststructuralism looks at history to illuminate how competing
social interests struggle over the meanings and associations pertaining to
signification. Several chapters in this book feature lesson plans that explore
some of these ideas. One of the most accessible books I have found in this
difficult theoretical area is Cherryholmes (1988). I would also recommend

Weedon (1987) and Belsey (1980). For a discussion particularly relevant for ESL, see Peirce (1989, 1990).

3. Foucault wrote extensively on the interrelationship of knowledge and power (1982, 1977). He argued that what is considered 'true' knowledge is as much a product of social and institutional constraints as it is a result of 'discovery' in the natural world. Moreover, once 'true' knowledge was produced, people usually modified their actions and behaviours in light of what a new truth suggested or expected of them. Truth, therefore, often functions as a form of power, *producing* effects that actively encourage self-regulation and conformity on the part of individuals. According to Foucault:

> Truth is a thing of this world: it is produced only by virtue of multiple forms of constraint. And it induces regular effects of power. Each society has its regime of truth, its 'general politics' of truth: that is, the types of discourse which it accepts and makes function as true; the mechanisms and instances which enable one to distinguish true and false statements, the means by which each is sanctioned; the techniques and procedures accorded value in the acquisition of truth; the status of those who are charged saying what counts as true. (Foucault quoted in Bennett 1991, 19)

One anecdote comes to mind as illustration. Once during a class at university, a visiting scholar from China talked about an article he had written, which had been rejected for publication. He complained that it was rejected because he had not cited enough 'experts' to support his position. With complete sincerity, he told us that he spoke to the editor and suggested that if the journal published the article, he could become an 'expert' and there would then be no need to quote other authors, who were only 'saying the same thing' anyway. Why bother?

Why indeed. While some might find him naive or self-serving, my experiences in China suggest that my Chinese colleague was having genuine difficulties negotiating the discursive rules that construct academic 'truth' in our society. Certainly, one such rule is to be familiar with existing research. But this is only a partial truth, particularly in light of the vast and ever-proliferating array of academic publications, of which few scholars can adequately keep abreast. The implicit or unwritten rule here would be 'publish or perish.' If one is published or cited, then one has gained power in the currency of the academy. Mutual interests converge here and serve as powerful inducements for the aspiring graduate student to seek 'knowledge' via the pathways established by veteran scholars.

More importantly, playing the discursive game not only bears symbolic rewards, it also confers tangible material benefits: tenured professorships, publishing contracts, funding for travel and research, and so on. (see Lakoff 1990).

4. Critical educators rightly point out that the representation of history – particularly the idea that there is only *one* history, which describes a past 'reality' – often reflects the particular interests of dominant social groups and is intended to silence questions that might challenge the status quo. Challenging the accepted notion of a singular and immutable history is therefore an appropriate pedagogical activity, especially for minority students whose histories and experiences of learning are often invisible in the curricula.

In China, however, the depiction of past events challenged some of my assumptions concerning what it means to do critical work around the notion (or representation) of 'history.' The story of Comrade Lei Feng, killed by a falling pole, was an official piece of history that served to exemplify and exhort sacrifice on the part of all citizens. During my stay, which was at the height of economic liberalization under Deng Xiao Ping, an article appeared in the *People's Daily* newspaper that suggested that Lei Feng had in earlier times cherished personal possessions. I was very surprised at how a common historical text could be so casually transformed, and in direct contradiction of earlier political (i.e., proletarian) conventions in China. As noted by Erbaugh (1990), biographies in China are often written as moral models. If the moral and ideological conditions of the society change, then 'history' is culturally and politically permitted to conform to a new moral imperative. The irony here is that for Chinese students from the People's Republic, the plurality and mutability of history ('histories,' or 'her/stories' as suggested by feminists) may reference traditional forms of authority rather than offer new strategies for social change.

5. Several writers in critical pedagogy have a similar dialogic notion on how knowledge is formed and the role of the teacher in facilitating its accomplishment. Lusted offers some important insights: 'Knowledge is not produced in the intentions of those who believe they hold it, whether in the pen or in the voice. It is produced in the process of interaction, between writer and reader at the moment of reading, and between teacher and learner at the moment of classroom engagement. Knowledge is not the matter that is offered so much as the matter that is understood' (1986, 4). I would expand Lusted's observation by adding that knowledge can also be produced through reflection long after the 'moment of interaction' has

passed. As the quote suggests, teaching is an exploration of that which brings about understanding, and how we might use that knowledge to bring about a vision of a more tolerant and democratic society.

The requirements of such a teaching strategy are no longer narrowly constrained in perception and location. Authors such as Simon (1992, 1988) and Lusted (1986) use the concept of pedagogy to represent this expanded notion of knowledge and education. Pedagogy, according to Simon, 'is a practice within which one acts with the intent of provoking experience that will simultaneously organize and disorganize a variety of understandings of our natural and social world' (1992, 56). Experience, and the perception of experience, is a pedagogical terrain extending from the individual's common-sense assumptions to the position of educational practices within configurations of social power. No longer separable, conflicts and beliefs that form identity are linked to principles that organize society. In this perspective, contradictions are not just to be resolved but understood as a prerequisite for an empowering pedagogy.

6. Ashworth (1985, ch. 2) identifies three types of communities: 'geo-political communities' based on physical boundaries that have a political function; 'common interest communities' based on shared interests of history, language, culture, politics, or experience; and 'professional communities,' which she defines as groups that are concerned in some way with language instruction and may work directly with other community groups.

7. I am grateful to Professor Normand Frenette of OISE for stimulating thought on this distinction.

CHAPTER 2. Teaching politics in an ESL Classroom

1. The right time and place for explicit grammar instruction remains a controversial issue in ESL. In the *TESOL Journal* (1992/1993) version of this chapter, reference to explicit grammar instruction for this particular lesson was deleted at the request of the editors because it was felt inappropriate for the journal's readership. The most interesting aspect of this conventional wisdom is the underlying orthodoxy that *all* students are the same and should be taught or corrected the same way. Most of my initial training emphasized that corrections interfere with 'communicative' language learning; grammar should only be taught within an explicit lesson on a specific structure. After some time teaching, however, I found this approach unresponsive to the diversity of student learning experiences in my classrooms. For many students, the absence of corrections often creates more silence than participation. The teacher's ability and sincerity

may come into question and some students will no longer attend class. Also, for students who come from teacher-centred learning environments, the experience of asserting their voice in class is a departure of great magnitude. Thus the provision of corrections serves as a familiar way station along an adventure in unfamiliar territory. With this in mind, corrections of grammar or pronunciation are not arbitrarily given out or withheld. In any language-learning situation, communicative or structurally focused, I might find a need to clarify something, or a student might make a request for assistance with which I would comply.

One other consideration deserves comment. Our belief that grammar corrections might impede second language acquisition may have considerable validity in many situations. Such a teaching focus may reflect our own sociocultural biases regarding language, however. Wai-lim Yip offers an intriguing notion that might be considered when teaching Chinese students: 'The success of the Chinese poets in authenticating the fluctuations of concrete events ... their ability to preserve the multiple relationships in a kind of penumbra of indeterminateness, depends to a great extent on the sparseness of syntactical demands ... There is an inseparability of medium and poetry, of language and world view. How, then, can a language of rigid syntactical rules (such as Indo-European languages) successfully approximate a mode of presentation whose success depends on freedom from syntax?' (1986, 35).

Wai-lim Yip's comparative observation suggests that the role of grammar in meaning making and the importance that some theorists accord to it in applied linguistics may not be applicable to all ESL students. Whether explicit grammar instruction precedes or follows meaningful practice – deductively or inductively – or whether we should bother teaching grammar at all to facilitate acquisition, it remains a pedagogical debate formed from within the European linguistic tradition. In contrast to a world-view where the demands of syntax are sparse, ESL's obsession with appropriate correction may reflect the possibility that, in English, grammar (or form) imposes far greater 'demands' upon meaning potential than in Chinese and perhaps many other languages.

2. The interrelationship of context and meaning is another important area of focus in poststructuralism. The lessons in this chapter emphasized that textual meanings are contingent upon context (e.g., the meeting with the Grade 7s). But the reverse is also important to consider, as these last two activities demonstrate. That is, words or texts can *produce* new contexts (e.g., 'hordes'). Moreover, the older or familiar context associated with a word serves as a kind of residue that lingers around a word when it

is imposed upon a new situation and predisposes negative or positive feelings onto a situation. The French poststructuralist Jacques Derrida provides a relevant point 'Every sign, linguistic or nonlinguistic, spoken or written (in the usual sense of this opposition), as a small or large unity, can be cited, put between quotation marks; thereby it can break with every given context, and engender infinitely new contexts in an absolutely nonsaturable fashion' (1982, 20). The relationship between text and context is essentially dialogical (see ch. 6). The important pedagogical point for ESL students is to recognize and use both sides of the 'dialogue' when necessary. Sometimes this means learning to read the context of situations in which they find themselves in order to understand both what is being implied and what might be most effective in the specific situation. Alternatively, this also means using 'unusual' words and texts in certain situations to provoke new contexts and shift the frames of reference in which ideas and social interests are evaluated.

Finally, a poststructural understanding of language emphasizes the timeliness of dialogue. Students need to learn that the connotations, strong feelings, and emotions *around* words, metaphors, and texts change with time; they go into 'erasure,' according to Derrida, losing much of their evocative force when they become over-used or too familiar (witness the gradual decline of reference to the 'mother of all ...' anecdotes in North American media).

CHAPTER 3: Critical Practice for a Changing World of Work

1. One noteworthy example is the impressive work of teenager Craig Kielburger, whose efforts have focused attention on exploitative child labour practices in developing countries. Kielburger has successfully attracted global media attention and embarrassed many politicians and transnational corporations into addressing the conditions that force children to produce goods at a cost with which Canadian workers could never 'compete' (see Kenna 1997). Indeed, the effectiveness of Kielberger's campaign might be measured from the backlash it has evoked from sectors of the corporatist media in Canada.

2. The issue of what is or is not 'culture' never ceases to generate rigorous debate. While doing an undergraduate degree in social anthropology, I remember several professors and authors who held to the view that culture doesn't really exist. That is, culture isn't something fixed or permanent, nor is it something with which we are born – an ascribed status. Rather, culture represents a complex translation of economic conditions, the material needs

of life, that determine people's actions and beliefs in a given place (see the theory of 'cultural materialism' in Harris 1980).

My own feeling is that culture is heavily influenced by economy, but that it cannot be subordinated to economic explanations. Societies often participate in ritual practices that are in fact counterproductive or 'irrational' in classical economic terms. Moreover, people often act, culturally and socially, on their *perceptions* of their material reality as much as any absolute measure of what those conditions might be. So perceptions – defined and communicated through language – are 'real things' in that they are key to how people act upon and subsequently transform their physical, emotional, and communal environments (see Bhaskar 1989; Corson 1997; Eisenhart 1995; Harries-Jones 1995). For ESL teachers, this also suggests that language practices in the classroom are influential in the formation of 'new' cultural traditions, histories and solidarities that potentially improve students' opportunities for the future.

CHAPTER 4: Linking Dynamic Processes: Research, Identity, and Intonation

1. Nunan (1990, 63) characterizes 'action' research by its focus on knowledge 'for a particular situation or purpose.' Teachers would orient their research ideas to the conditions and problems that arise in their classroom. In this way they would generate theory with which to customize the curriculum for their particular circumstances. Erickson (1986) points out that 'qualitative' research in education involves participant observation and interpretation in the classroom. It is often contrasted with quantitative research, which tends towards techniques of scientific collection and measurement to generate theory. Both authors point out the need to situate research in the social context where theoretical insights can directly inform teaching (see also Lynch 1996 for an excellent discussion of quantitative and qualitative research and evaluation in language programs from both positivistic and naturalistic perspectives.)

2. An interesting example can be found in Day's (1990) suggestions for doing classroom ethnography. In a section on 'techniques and instruments for observation,' he suggests that 'the written statements in an ethnography should be as descriptive and objective as possible, and *should not be judgmental or evaluative*' (45, emphasis mine). Later, he warns that tired student teachers may 'fail to keep an accurate record of events' and that 'the anecdotal record or written ethnography may be affected by the biases of the student teacher' (46). Finally, near the end of this subsection on qualitative approaches, Day adds that 'what is perceived is heavily

influenced by the observer's own experiences. It is difficult to be objective
and neutral' (46). What I find significant in these latter qualifications
is that, by their location and tone, how they detract only superficially
from the general implication that a place of objective accuracy, free from
personal judgement, bias, and evaluation, is not only attainable but, more
importantly, desirable in classroom ethnography. Failure to achieve the
desired goal of 'objectivity' is one of application not of premise. Perhaps
an equally important research question might be, 'To what extent is the
need for "techniques" and "instruments" particular to the culture of the
ethnographer?' or 'What are the underlying discourses and power relations
that privilege detachment, neutrality, and objectivity as valued forms of
knowledge?'

3. Such possibilities are eloquently corroborated in Giltrow and Calhoun's
(1992) provocative article on Mayan resistance to ESL orthodoxy: 'While
we have learned a little about their assumptions, they have learned a lot
about ours. They have learned that, in this community where English is
the first language of most people, institutional/cultural traditions value
practices which trigger language behavior and capture it for the purpose of
measuring its deviation from a norm. They reject this tradition and resist'
(62).

4. Halliday's approach emphasizes that social context is not something
'external' to language but rather encoded at the sentence and clausal level.
A 'functional' grammar (Halliday and Hasan 1985) describes language, or
texts, as simultaneously operating in several environments while utilizing
a singular surface form of lexical, grammatical, and phonological elements.
A text has both internal *cohesion*, how it is assembled in terms of semantic
and structural relationships, as well as external cohesiveness reflecting the
specific 'context of situation' in which it is realized as spoken or written
language. Halliday's notion of register is concerned with how we are able
to make appropriate language choices – in terms of text and context – for a
wide range of social situations, in turn influenced by larger cultural norms
and expectations (ibid.).

5. Most researchers today would incorporate social identity as a variable
for second language acquisition. They would anticipate differences based
on the influence of *family, gender, race,* or *culture,* for example. But where
would these differences actually reside: in the performance of students or
as an inadvertent consequence of the theoretical framework that had been
applied? It is important to remember that our profession has traditionally
relied upon conceptual tools that decontextualize, generalize, and objectify
data. Such research techniques implicitly support a notion of identity as

insular and static, passed down intact over time and across locations. But family, gender, race, or culture – unlike grammar or the functioning of the brain – may not be general or stable theoretical categories. The key point in this chapter is that they may be contingent notions, undergoing change and inscribed with relations of power that reflect local contexts and particular histories (see Bourne 1988; Cummins 1996; Peirce 1995). These are the types of conditions in which prescribed methods for doing classroom research are less likely to assist teachers.

6. An important point here is that the reasons for classroom silence or resistance are complex and rarely self-evident (Schenke 1991); one such cause can be a reluctance to transgress linguistic, cultural, gendered, and classed norms that sustain supportive social networks in a competitive and impersonal economy often hostile to newcomers (see Goldstein 1997).

7. It is important to note that Halliday's theoretical work has been criticized for being somewhat deterministic and unable to account for social agency, language change, and the divergent and idiosyncratic choices that individuals make in their language use (see O'Donnell and Todd 1991; Clark 1992). This is a concern easily and justifiably applied to almost all functionalist theories of society and descriptive grammars as well, particularly since Saussure's detemporalized (i.e., synchronic) and homogeneous (i.e., *la langue*) treatment of linguistic analysis (see Howatt 1984). Anytime we identify function through form and form through function, there is the potential of overlooking or simplifying complex social and ideological processes that shape the experience of identity but are not directly encoded or materially evident in texts. And in the classroom, there is the attendant danger of objectifying a singular form/function relationship and using it normatively when instructing or evaluating students.

It seems to me, though, that there are elements of Halliday and Hasan's (1985) work that do account for linguistic innovation and social agency. The discussion of intonation in this chapter may be one example. It is probable that the use of a particular intonation pattern to achieve particular social goals surreptitiously would have timely and limited use. As a text, it might soon lose its intended ambiguity and become the context against which future 'deceptive' utterances would be formed and evaluated (a feature of 'intertextuality,' Halliday and Hasan 1985, 47). As noted by Halliday (47), new meanings arise from the 'friction' between text and context and within the larger context of culture. This relationship is inherently dialectical: patterns of regularity influence variations, which, in turn, can cumulatively transform prior norms in linguistic communities.

CHAPTER 6: A Dangerous Future

1. Lakoff (1990, 207–9) shows that for women to enter the echelons of male power, such as in business or politics, they are required to 'code switch' (see Heller 1988). Essentially, they must begin to talk and act like powerful men – a kind of 'no-win' situation where they are judged either 'too aggressive' (i.e., 'non-womanly'), or 'not tough enough' to make 'difficult' decisions. By code switching, women also lose the opportunity to introduce alternative forms of consensual and non-hierarchical ways of being and knowing into traditionally male institutions.

2. In Lakoff's perspective, 'powerful' language is not a universal or innate capacity transferred along with other genetic material. What language does, and the ways in which powerful men have regulated its forms and uses, are socially and historically situated. Lakoff (1990, 203) offers as example the Malagasy Republic, where women and men have been socialized to speak in ways that reverse the discourse strategies that characterize gendered speech in our own society. Lakoff's observation poses another important challenge for feminist pedagogy. Once we recognize that gendered language is *socially* produced, we cannot assume that exclusionary or coercive language practices necessarily change when women attain positions of power. Whether based on gender, race, class, or culture, oppressed social groups are equally capable of becoming oppressors in spite of past experiences and assumed positions of solidarity.

3. Marylin Waring (1988) offers a powerful and detailed discussion of how the language of economics has arbitrarily rendered women 'economically inactive' and how this devaluation is achieved through mathematical formulas that 'assist in the illusion' of a value-free economics. This is not just a case of semantics or terminology. When women's work is deemed 'valueless' by agencies such as the World Bank or IMF, then policies get set into motion which make conditions in the developing world more severe (see also Cummins 1996; Simon 1992).

4. In critical pedagogy, personal experience is a site of resistance and empowerment for marginalized social groups (see Cummins 1989a). Institutions of government, education, or the law value ways of knowing and learning that closely parallel the values of dominant groups in a given society. Such dominant values are depicted as 'natural' and necessary for success in the society. Consequently, 'alternative' experiences of learning are discouraged, because it is assumed that they will impair progress and integration into the mainstream. Writers in critical pedagogy reject this assumption and its underlying intent to assimilate and control

minority groups. There are many ways of knowing and learning that, when encouraged and developed in the classroom, facilitate minority educational and social achievement and subsequently enrich the greater society.

5. As noted by Waring (1988), if one wants to argue with an economist that orthodox economics discriminates against women, one is forced to 'prove' such assertions by using classical economic models or 'facts' – an underlying *cause* of the problem. If one doesn't use such models, economists will reply that the argument is 'irrational,' in economic terms, and thus not worth their serious consideration.

6. Lakoff (1990, ch. 13) provides an excellent discussion on the contingencies of time and place for effective rhetorical strategies by analysing and comparing the oratory of Julius Caesar with Oliver North.

7. In the perspective of this chapter, one might also consider the notion of grammar as a masculine discourse organized on the same gendered principles as economics or politics. From the early structuralism of de Saussure in the late nineteenth century to the transformational-generative grammar of Chomsky, modern linguistics has attempted to treat grammar as an objective, timeless, and decontextualized entity not unlike a 'calculus.' It's interesting to speculate on what the priorities of a feminist grammar or applied linguistics might be. In the classroom, similar to this lesson, a teacher might approach 'structural' analyses as if they were interconnected with the emotional meanings generated from a given reading; that is, the concreteness of description might be considered from the point of reception. In this way, grammar would be socially contingent, even *personalized*, at the moment a text was read and thus potentially multiple in form.

References

Allen, J.P.B. 1983. A three-level curriculum model for second-language education. *The Canadian Modern Language Review* 40(1): 23–43.

Allen, J.P.B., M. Swain, B. Harley, and J. Cummins. 1990. Aspects of classroom treatment: Toward a more comprehensive view of second language education. In *The development of second language proficiency*, ed. B. Harley, P. Allen, J. Cummins, and M. Swain, 57–81. Cambridge: Cambridge University Press.

Ashworth, M. 1985. *Beyond methodology: Second language teaching and the community*. Cambridge: Cambridge University Press.

Auerbach, E.R. 1993. Reexamining English only in the ESL classroom. *TESOL Quarterly* 27(1): 9–30.

Auerbach, E.R., and L. McGrail. 1991. Rosa's challenge: Connecting classroom and community contexts. In *ESL in America: Myths and possibilities*, ed. Sarah Benesch, 96–111. Portsmouth, NH: Boynton/Cook.

Auerbach, E.R., and N. Wallerstein. 1987. *ESL for action: Problem-posing at work*. Reading, MA: Addison-Wesley.

Avery, P., and S. Ehrlich. 1992. *Teaching American English pronunciation*. Oxford: Oxford University Press.

Bander, R. 1980. *From sentence to paragraph: A workbook in English as a second language*. New York: Holt, Rinehart and Winston.

Bateson, G. 1972. *Steps to an ecology of mind*. New York: Ballantine Books.

Beisbeir, B. 1995. *Sounds great: Intermediate pronunciation and speaking for learners of English*, vol. 2. Boston, MA: Heinle and Heinle.

Bell, J. 1991. Becoming aware of literacy. Ph.D. dissertation, OISE/University of Toronto.

– 1995. The Relationship between L1 and L2 literacy: Some complicating factors. *TESOL Quarterly* 29(4): 687–704.

Belsey, C. 1980. *Critical practice*. New York: Methuen.

Benesch, S. ed. 1991. *ESL in America: Myths and possibilities*. Portsmouth, NH: Boynton/Cook, Heinemann.

– 1994. ESL, ideology, and the politics of pragmatics. *TESOL Quarterly* 27(4): 705–16.

Bennett, A. 1991. Discourses of power, the dialectics of understanding, the power of literacy. In *Rewriting literacy: Culture and discourse of the other*, ed. C. Mitchell, and K. Weiler, 13–33. Toronto: OISE Press.

Bhaskar, R. 1989. *Reclaiming reality: A critical introduction to contemporary philosophy*. London: Verso.

Boissevain, J. 1985. Networks. In *The social science encyclopedia*, ed. A. Kuper and J. Kuper, 557–8. London: Routledge.

Botha, R. 1989. *Challenging Chomsky: The generative garden game*. Oxford: Basil Blackwell.

Bourne, J. 1988. 'Natural acquisition' and a 'masked pedagogy'. *Applied Linguistics* 9(1): 83–99.

Bowers, B., and J. Godfrey. 1985. *Decisions, decisions*. Agincourt, Ont: Dominie Press.

Brumfit, C.J., and Johnson, K. ed. 1979. *The communicative approach to language teaching*. Oxford: Oxford University Press.

Burnaby, B. 1992. Co-ordinating settlement services: Why is it so difficult? In *Socio-political aspects of ESL*, ed. B. Burnaby and A. Cumming, 122–37. Toronto: OISE Press.

Burnaby, B., and A. Cumming. ed. 1992. *Socio-political aspects of ESL*. Toronto: OISE Press.

Canagarajah, A.S. 1993. Critical ethnography of a Sri Lankan classroom: Ambiguities in opposition to reproduction through TESOL. *TESOL Quarterly* 27(4): 601–26.

– 1996. From critical research practice to critical research reporting. *TESOL Quarterly* 30(2): 321–31.

– in press. *Resistance in English language teaching: Ethnographies from the periphery*. Oxford: Oxford University Press.

Canale, M., and M. Swain. 1980. Theoretical bases of communicative approaches to second language teaching and testing. *Applied Linguistics* 1(1): 1–47.

Celce-Murcia, M., and D. Larsen-Freeman. 1983. *The grammar book: An ESL/EFL teacher's course*. London: Newbury House Publishers.

Cherryholmes, C. 1988. *Power and criticism: Poststructuralist investigations in education*. New York: Teachers College Press.

– 1993. Reading research. *Journal of Curriculum Studies* 25(1): 1–32.

Chow, R. 1992. Between colonizers: Hong Kong's postcolonial self-writing in the 1990s. *Diaspora* 2(2): 151–70.

Clark, R. 1992. Principles and practice of CLA in the classroom. In *Critical language awareness*, ed. N. Fairclough. 117–40. New York: Longman.

Clark, R., N. Fairclough, R. Ivanic, and M. Martin-Jones. 1990. Critical language awareness, part 1: A critical review of three current approaches to language awareness. *Language and Education* 4: 249–60.

– 1991. Critical language awareness, part 2: Towards critical alternatives. *Language and Education* 5: 41–54.

Clarke, M. 1994. The dysfunctions of the theory/practice discourse. *TESOL Quarterly* 28(1): 9–26.

Clifford, J. 1988. *The predicament of culture*. Cambridge: Harvard University Press.

Cooke, D. 1987. Ties that constrict: English as a Trojan horse. In *Awareness: Proceedings of the 1987 TESL Ontario Conference*, ed. A. Cumming, A. Gagne, and J. Dawson, 56–62. Toronto: TESL Ontario.

– 1988. Language with strings attached. In *TESL'88: Raising the profile. Proceedings of the 1988 TESL Ontario Conference*, ed. E. Harris, and H. McGarrell, 27–35. Toronto: TESL Ontario.

– 1993. Just add power (response to Sheila Sage). *TESL Talk* 21: 88–98.

Corson, D. 1993. *Language, minority education and gender: Linking social justice and power*. Toronto: OISE Press.

– 1997. Critical realism: An emancipatory philosophy for applied linguistics? *Applied Linguistics* 18(2): 166–88.

Covey, M. 1983. Cultural conventions and expectations of two cultural groups in reading and writing. Master's thesis, OISE/University of Toronto.

Crystal, D. 1987. *The Cambridge encyclopedia of language*. New York: Cambridge University Press.

Cumming, A. ed. 1994. Alternatives in TESOL research: Descriptive, interpretive, and ideological orientations. *TESOL Quarterly* 28(4): 673–704.

Cummins, J. 1989a. *Empowering minority students*. Sacramento, CA: California Association for Bilingual Education.

– 1989b. The sanitized curriculum: Educational disempowerment in a nation at risk. In *Richness in writing: Empowering ESL students*, ed. D. Johnson and D. Roen, 19–38. New York: Longman.

– 1990. Reflections on 'empowerment.' *CABE Newsletter*, 12(3): 7, 11.

– 1993a. Negotiating identities in the ESL classroom. *Contact* 19(1): 30–2.

– 1993b. Plenary address, tenth annual colloquium: Theory and practice in the classroom. Brock University, St. Catharines, Ont.

– 1996. *Negotiating identities: Education for empowerment in a diverse society.* Ontario, CA: California Association for Bilingual Education.

Cummins, J., and L. Cameron. 1994. The ESL student *is* the mainstream: The marginalization of diversity in current Canadian educational debates. *English Quarterly* 26(3): 30–3.

Davin, D. 1976. *Woman-work.* Oxford: Clarendon Press.

Day, R. 1990. Teacher observation in second language teacher education. In *Second language teacher education,* ed. D. Nunan and J. Richards, 43–61. Cambridge: Cambridge University Press.

Derrida, J. 1982. *Margins of philosophy.* trans. A. Bass. Chicago: University of Chicago Press.

Dillon, P. 1986. Process writing. B.Ed. thesis, Brock University, St. Catherine's Ont.

Dufficy, P. 1993. The pedagogy of pre-service TESOL teacher education. *Journal of Education for Teaching: International Research and Pedagogy* 19(1): 83–96.

Eisenhart, M. 1995. The fax, the jazz player, and the self-story teller: How *do* people organize culture? *Anthropology and Education Quarterly* 26(1): 3–26.

Ekins, P., M. Hillman, and R. Hutchison. 1992. *The gaia atlas of green economics.* Toronto: Anchor Books.

Elson, N. 1989. The teacher as a participating citizen. *TESL Talk* 19(1): 47–55.

Elvin, M. 1991. The inner world of 1830. *Dædalus* 120(2): 33–63.

Erbaugh, M. 1990. Taking advantage of China's literary tradition in teaching Chinese students. *The Modern Language Journal* 74(i): 15–27.

Erickson, F. 1986. Qualitative methods in research on teaching. In *Handbook of research on teaching,* ed. M. Wittlock, 119–61. New York: Macmillan.

Fairclough, N. ed. 1992. *Critical language awareness.* New York: Longman.

Faltis, C., and S. Hudelson. 1994. Learning English as an additional language in K-12 schools. *TESOL Quarterly* 28(3): 457–68.

Foucault, M. 1977. *Discipline and punish: The birth of the prison.* trans. A. Sheridan. New York: Vantage Books.

– 1982. The subject and power. In *Michel Foucault: Beyond structuralism and hermeneutics,* ed. H. Dreyfus and P. Rabinow, 208–26. Chicago: University of Chicago Press.

Freire, P. 1973. *Education for critical consciousness.* New York: Seabury Press.

– 1974. *Pedagogy of the oppressed.* New York: Seabury Press.

Galbraith, J. 1992. *The culture of contentment.* New York: Houghton Mifflin.

Gardner, R., and W. Lambert 1972. *Attitudes and motivation in second-language learning.* Rowley, MA: Newbury House.

Geertz, C. 1983. *Local knowledge*. New York: Basic Books.

Gilbert, J. 1993. *Clear speech: Pronunciation and listening comprehension in North American English*, 2nd ed. Cambridge: Cambridge University Press.

Giltrow, J. and E.R. Calhoun. 1992. The culture of power: ESL traditions, Mayan resistance. In *Socio-political aspects of ESL*, ed. B. Burnaby and A. Cumming, 50–66. Toronto: OISE Press.

Giroux, H. 1988. *Schooling and the struggle for public life: Critical pedagogy in the modern age*. Minneapolis: University of Minnesota Press.

– 1994. Doing cultural studies: Youth and the challenge of pedagogy. *Harvard Educational Review* 64(3): 278–308.

Goldstein, T. 1994. 'We are sisters, so we don't have to be polite': Language choice and English language training in the multilingual workplace. *TESL Canada Journal* 11(2): 30–45.

– 1997. *Two languages at work: Bilingual life on the production floor*. Hawthorne, NY: Walter de Gruyter.

Halliday, M.A.K. 1985. *Spoken and written language*. Oxford: Oxford University Press.

Halliday, M.A.K., and R. Hasan. 1985. *Language, context, and text: aspects of language in a social-semiotic perspective*. Oxford: Oxford University Press.

Harries-Jones, P. 1995. *A recursive vision: Ecological understanding and Gregory Bateson*. Toronto: University of Toronto Press.

Harris, M. 1980. *Culture, people, nature: An introduction to general anthropology*. New York: Harper and Row.

Hats on! 1992. *Time*, 17 February: 162.

Heller, M. ed. 1988. *Codeswitching: Anthropological and sociolinguistic perspectives*. New York: Mouton de Gruyter.

Howatt, A.P.R. 1984. *A history of English language teaching*. Oxford: Oxford University Press.

Hunter, J., and D. Cooke. 1988. Dealing with argument: Content and skills in ESL. In *TESL'88: Raising the profile. Proceedings of the 1988 TESL Ontario Conference*, ed. E. Harris and H. McGarrell, 103–10. Toronto: TESL Ontario.

Hynes, M., M. Belfiore, D. Cooke, F. Gorbet, and P. Parsons. 1982. Can you succeed overseas? *TESL Talk* 13(3): 28–44.

Janks, H. 1993. *Language and position*. Critical Language Awareness Series, ed. H. Janks. Johannesburg: Witwatersrand University Press.

– 1989. Critical linguistics: A starting point for oppositional reading. Paper presented at the Annual Boston University Conference on Language Development, October, Boston, MA. (ERIC Document Reproduction Service No. ED314 942.)

Jingoism: Mad dogs and Englishmen. 1991. *Globe and Mail*, 23 February: D5.

Kenna, K. 1997. Clinton launches war on world sweatshops. *Toronto Star*, 15 April: A16.

King, A.Y. 1991. Kuan-hsi and network building: A sociological interpretation. *Daedalus* 120(2): 63–84.

Krashen, S. 1988. *Second language acquisition and second language learning.* New York: Prentice Hall.

Kress, G. 1991. Critical discourse analysis. *Annual Review of Applied Linguistics* 11: 84–99.

Kreidler, C. 1989. *The pronunciation of English: A course book in phonology.* Oxford: Blackwell Publishers.

Kuper, A. 1973. *Anthropologists and anthropology: The British school 1922–72.* New York: Penguin Books.

Lakoff, R. 1990. *Talking power: The politics of language.* New York: Basic Books.

Lemke, J.L. 1987. Social semiotics and science education. *The American Journal of Semiotics* 5(2): 217–32.

– 1989. Semantics and social values. *Word* 40(1/2): 37–50.

Li Xiao Ping. 1987. Women's studies in China: Just the beginning. Unpublished manuscript. York University.

Lucas, T., and A. Katz. 1994. Reframing the debate: The roles of native languages in English-only programs for language minority students. *TESOL Quarterly* 28(3): 537–61.

Lusted, D. 1986. Why pedagogy? *Screen* 27(5): 2–14.

Lynch, B.K. 1996. *Language program evaluation: Theory and practice.* Cambridge: Cambridge University Press.

Mallet, G. 1993. Murder at the Kim Bo. *Toronto Life*, February, 32–8.

Matalene, C. 1985. Contrastive rhetoric: An American writing teacher in China. *College English* 47(8): 789–807.

McGarrell, H. 1992. Peer feedback in writing classes. In *TESL'91: Make changes/Make a difference*, ed. G. Irons and T.S. Paribakht, 131–8. Welland, Ont.: Editions Soleil Publishing.

McLaren, P. 1989. *Life in schools: An introduction to critical pedagogy in the foundations of education.* New York: Longman.

McLaren, P., and P. Leonard. ed. 1993. *Paulo Freire: A critical encounter.* London: Routledge.

McKay, S. 1989. Topic development and written discourse accent. In *Richness in writing: Empowering ESL students*, ed. D. Johnson and D. Roen, 253–62. New York: Longman.

Mittan, R. 1989. The peer review process: Harnessing students' communicative power. In *Richness in writing: Empowering ESL students*, ed. D. Johnson and D. Roen, 207–19. New York: Longman.

Moloney, K. 1991. Values, world views, ideology and ESL. Paper presented at TESL Ontario Annual Conference, Toronto, Ontario, 21–23 August.

Morgan, B. ed. 1991. *Stories from our class: A collection of adult ESL compositions.* vol. 1. Toronto: St. Steven's Community House.

– ed. 1992. *Stories from our class: A collection of adult ESL compositions.* vol. 2. Toronto: St. Steven's Community House.

– 1992/1993. Teaching the Gulf War in an ESL classroom. *TESOL Journal* 2(2): 13–7.

– 1996a. Promoting and assessing critical language awareness. *TESOL Journal* 5(2): 10–14.

– 1996b. Exploring bilingualism in a community-based ESL program. *Bilingual Basics* (Fall): 6–8.

– 1997a. The politics of publishing: Positioning critical voices in an ELT Journal. *College ESL* 7(1): 14–31.

– 1997b. Challenging fiscal constraints through a community-based pedagogy. In *Proceedings of TESL Canada at the Learned Societies' Congress*, Brock University, 1996, ed. J. Cleland and J. Sivell. TESL Canada (www.tesl.ca)

Morgan, R.G. 1991. Beaver ecology/beaver mythology. Ph.D. dissertation, University of Alberta.

Morley, J. 1991. The pronunciation component in teaching English to speakers of other languages. *TESOL Quarterly* 25(3): 481–520.

Murphy, J. 1991. Oral communication in TESOL: Integrating speaking, listening and pronunciation. *TESOL Quarterly* 25(1): 51–76.

Naiman, N. 1992. A communicative approach to pronunciation teaching. In *Teaching American English pronunciation*, ed. P. Avery and S. Ehrlich, 163–71. Oxford: Oxford University Press.

Nayar, P.B. 1997. ESL/EFL dichotomy today: Language politics or pragmatics. *TESOL Quarterly* 31(1): 9–37.

Ng, R. 1989. Sexism, racism, and Canadian nationalism. *Socialist Studies/Etudes Socialistes: A Canadian Annual* 5: 10–25.

Nunan, D. 1988. *Syllabus design.* Oxford: Oxford University Press.

– 1990. Action research in the language classroom. In *Second language teacher education*, ed. D. Nunan and J. Richards, 43–61. Cambridge: Cambridge University Press.

Nunan, D., and J.C. Richards. ed. 1990. *Second language teacher education.* Cambridge: Cambridge University Press.

O'Donnell, W.R., and L. Todd. 1991. *Variety in contemporary English*. New York: HarperCollins.

O'Malley, S. 1991. Men, teens sought after 3 shot dead. *Globe and Mail*, 4 March: A4.

Peirce, B.N. 1989. Toward a pedagogy of possibility in the teaching of English internationally. *TESOL Quarterly* 23(3): 401–20.

– 1990. Comments on 'Toward a pedagogy of possibility in the teaching of English internationally: People's English in South Africa': The author responds. *TESOL Quarterly* 24(1): 105–12.

– 1994. Using diaries in second language research and teaching. *English Quarterly* 26(3): 22–9.

– 1995. Social identity, investment, and language learning. *TESOL Quarterly* 29(1): 9–30.

Pennycook, A. 1989. The concept of method, interested knowledge, and the politics of language teaching. *TESOL Quarterly* 23(4): 589–617.

– 1990. Critical pedagogy and second language education. *System* 18(3): 303–14.

– 1994a. *The cultural politics of English as an international language*. London: Longman.

– 1994b. Incommensurable discourses? *Applied Linguistics* 15: 115–38.

Phillipson, R. 1992. *Linguistic imperialism*. Oxford: Oxford University Press.

Plant, J. 1990. Searching for common ground: Ecofeminism and bioregionalism. In *Home! A bioregional reader*, ed. V. Andruss, C. Plant, J. Plant, and E. Wright, 79–82. Philadelphia: New Society Publishers.

Podoliak, E. ed. 1993. *TESL Talk: ESL in the changing world of work*. vol. 21. Toronto: Ontario Ministry of Citizenship.

Rockhill, K., and P. Tomic. 1994. There is a connection: Racism, hetero/sexism and access to ESL. *Canadian Woman Studies/Les cahiers de la femme* 14(2): 91–4.

Said, E. 1978. *Orientalism*. New York: Vintage Books.

Sahlins, M. 1972. *Stone age economics*. Chicago: Aldine Publishing.

Saul, J.R. 1992. *Voltaire's bastards: The dictatorship of reason in the west*. New York: The Free Press.

Schenke, A. 1991. The 'Will to Reciprocity' and the work of memory: Fictioning speaking out of silence in ESL and feminist pedagogy. *Resources for Feminist Research* 20: 47–55.

Scholes, R. 1985. *Textual power*. New Haven, Conn.: Yale University Press.

Shor, I. 1992. *Empowering education: Critical teaching for social change*. Chicago: University of Chicago Press.

Siebers, T. 1988. *The ethics of criticism*. Ithaca, NY: Cornell University Press.

Simon, R. 1987. Being ethnic/Doing ethnicity: A response to Corrigan. In *Breaking the mosaic: Ethnic identities in Canadian schooling*, ed. J. Young, 31–44. Toronto: Garamond Press.

– 1988. For a pedagogy of possibility. *Critical Pedagogy Networker* 1(1): 1–4.

– 1992. *Teaching against the grain*. Toronto: OISE Press.

Simon, R., D. Dippo, and A. Schenke. 1991. *Learning work: A critical pedagogy of work education*. Toronto: OISE Press.

Stern, H. 1997. Confessions of an ESL Revolutionary. Adult Education Newsletter. *TESOL* (Spring): 5–6.

Students of Jarvis Collegiate. 1983. *Search for self: Thoughts and feelings of new Canadian teenagers*, ed. J. Porter. Toronto: Toronto Board of Education. Reprint, 1991. *New Canadian voices*. Toronto: Wall and Emerson.

Sun-risk warnings begin next month. 1992. *Toronto Star*, 20 February: A5.

Swain, M. 1984. Teaching and testing communicatively. *TESL Talk* 15(1/2): 7–18.

Thompson, A. 1993. 'Astronauts' at home here but work in Hong Kong. *Toronto Star*, 20 April: A1, A24.

2 top Bata executives fined for polluting. 1992. *Toronto Star*, 7 April: A3.

Tyler, T. 1993. Judge hears 'blunt' facts about racism. *The Toronto Star*, 13 April: A2.

U.S. risks world's future, Strong says. 1992. *Toronto Star*, 12 March: A3.

Vandrick, S. 1997. The role of hidden identities in the postsecondary ESL classroom. *TESOL Quarterly* 31(1): 153–7.

van Lier, L. 1994. Forks and hope: Pursuing understanding in different ways. *Applied Linguistics* 15(3): 328–46.

Wallerstein, N. 1983. The teaching approach of Paulo Freire. In *Methods that work: A smorgasbord of ideas for language teachers*, ed. J.W. Oller, Jr., and P.A. Richard-Amato, 190–204. Rowley, MA: Newbury House.

Waring, M. 1988. *If women counted*. San Francisco: HarperCollins.

Watson, P. 1991. Foreign-born workers keep Metro moving. *Toronto Star*, 21 September: A1, A8.

Weedon, C. 1987. *Feminist practice & poststructuralist theory*. New York: Basil Blackwell.

Weiler, K. 1991. Freire and a feminist pedagogy of difference. *Harvard Educational Review* 61(4): 449–74.

Weiler, K., and C. Mitchell. ed. 1992. *What schools can do: Critical pedagogy and practice*. New York: SUNY Press.

Wells, G. 1987. Apprenticeship in literacy. *Interchange* 18(1/2): 109–23.

Wodak, R. 1990. Discourse analysis: Problems, findings, perspectives. *Text* 10(1/2): 125–32.

Yang, L. 1957. The concept of *pao* as a basis for social relations. In *Chinese thoughts and institutions*, ed. J. Fairbank, 291–309. Chicago: University of Chicago Press.

Yates, L. 1992. Postmodernism, feminism, and cultural politics: Or, if master narratives have been discredited, what does Giroux think he is doing? *Discourse* 13(1):124–33.

Yip, W. 1986. The framing of critical theories: A reconsideration. *Asian Culture Quarterly* 14(3): 30–7.

Index